CW01501983

Copyright © 2010 by Sedick Isaacs
Third print

ISBN: Softcover   978-1-4535-3806-7
       e-Book   978-1-4535-3807-4

First published by XLibris

This book was printed in South Africa

To order additional copies contact:
  Mrs M. Isaacs tel 083-512 4997
  Or email: si88364@gmail.com

Contents

Preface …………………………...…………………………….………..9

Chapter 1:   *The Prior years*…………………………………………16

Chapter 2:   *Arrest*……………………………………………………27

Chapter 3:   *Devils Island* ……………………………………………47

Chapter 4   *First Day in the Yard* ……………………………………77

Chapter 5:   *Hard labour in the Quarry* ……………………………87

Chapter 6:   *Cell Life* …………………………………………………118

Chapter 7:   *Prison Protest* …………………………………………137

Chapter 8:   *Solitary Confinement on Robben Island* ……146

Chapter 9:   *Getting Educated* ………………………………………175

Chapter 10:.. *Sport and recreation* …………………………………198

Chapter 11:   *The Master key* ………………………………………216

Chapter 12:   *C onquering the quarry* ………………………………224

Chapter 13:   *Release and Banned* …………………………………230

Surviving in the Apartheid Prison:
Robben Island

In loving memory of Sadick Isaacs
a Comerade, loving father, and
Grandfather and devoted
husband to Maraldea.

Thank you for your support

Maraldea
1/2/2014

Surviving in the Apartheid Prison: Robben Island

Flashbacks of an earlier life

Sedick Isaacs

Dedication

This book is dedicated to my mother who shared the burden of police searches, arrest and courts and to my wife Maraldea, my daughters Nadia and Wanita who shared the years of Banning orders, prohibitions and more courts.

Preface

I have now finally allowed myself to be persuaded to put my Island experiences in writing. Some of the experiences there are, even to day, still painful and still, in some inexplicable way, embarrassing and not easy to talk about. I have therefore had thus far not much inclination to write or talk about these experiences even against very flattering arguments mentioned by historians and comrades such as that I must have, by my activities, "touched on the lives of almost every Robben Island prisoner of the period" during my stay there. I was up to now too busy trying to catch up with a career, teaching, running a company and coaching the sons and daughters of my friends and family who had difficulties with Mathematics. Besides this, most of the events I experienced still felt a bit too raw even after so many years. There are consequently gaps in my memory. I still have bouts of feelings of isolation and loneliness even in the midst of family and friends and again I cannot explain this. .Even now that it has been written and completed I still hesitate sending it to the printer.

Right from the onset I want to point out that this is not a political analysis of the times but a simple narrative. The political analysis and commentary may be done in another work. I will try and keep the narrative and observations as clinical as possible although I know this will not be easy.

I think I had a particularly rough time on Robben Island when compared to my fellow prisoners whose lives there were less eventful. Even Nelson Mandela had a very even life in prison. I, on the other hand, seemed to have attracted unnecessary attention from the warders and their authorities. I was, with Achmad Cassiem, often singled out and derided as an 'amper baas' (almost boss or almost white), I had the unfortunate distinction of having gone through long terms of solitary confinement (not just single cell accommodation) and in 1965 I spent almost a year in solitary confinement. I was, I think, the only one who had an extensive addition to my sentence for prison 'offences'. The other person who I know had an addition was Michael Maimane who had a month added. Reading through my prison records kept in the National Archives I learnt that the Security Police was at one time seriously considering a further charge of sabotage with the possibility of adding at least another fifteen years to my sentence arising out of some of my activities in Robben Island Prison. The events leading to these I will recount in this narrative. I was further never awarded the 'luxury' of becoming a privileged 'A Grade or Group' prisoner until the last few month of my sentence.

'Promotion' in prison from the under privileged D grade to the privileged A-group was dependent on what the prison authorities classed as 'good behaviour' and as 'security prisoners' we all entered as D-groups in contrast to common law prisoners who entered as C-groups. At one stage I was told that I was demoted to an E-group for 'poor behaviour' even though the lowest classification level in terms of the Prison Regulations was a D and yet I considered my behaviour as having always been at its very best. I was further assaulted (which some others also experienced) resulting in dislocation of my jaw and a split lip. I had chains put on my wrist, waist and ankles and left naked in damp and cold solitary confinement cell. On another occasion I was strapped by my wrist and ankles onto a wooden frame and flogged for 'insulting' the Prison Department: a degrading 'punishment' out of the 18th century. It is indeed fortunate that the human memory does not carry raw physical pain. Unfortunately memory does, for me, carry psychological pain and also the pain of continuous unrelenting cold that I experienced in the solitary cells which lead to hypothermia when shivering stops and the jaw clamps up tight leading to a type of convulsive and uncontrollable flexing and extension of all the muscles of the body as the organism desperately tried to generate heat. Freezing in the labour quarry during winter sitting down and breaking stones on the 'nap line' exposed to the biting Atlantic sea spray was another is another experience in cryotherapy and   an experience I have difficulty erasing from memory.   I still find myself fearing cold with an almost pathological reflex. Hell for me is certainly a cold place. I live in Cape Town and with every winter I cannot help thinking of moving to the warmer city of Durban.

On the other hand I think I also had achievements on Robben Island.   I tutored students who did well and became prominent persons after their release. I helped prisoners with physical as well as rather difficult mental health problems; I expanded our sport and recreation, and helped develop and promoted our cultural lives in prison. I completed three university degrees through correspondence at the University of South Africa, learnt computing and single handed restructured the Prison Library classifying the collection in the Dewey system and constructing the Prison library catalogue. I also helped with a research project that became the basis of a theology thesis and started a research project of my own to investigate a theory why some people are susceptible to sea sickness by studying the transmission of sensory information across sensory modalities using my fellow prisoners as subjects. I had first hand experience with what I called 'eventless time'. I also worked on the factors that make up human physical fitness by observing and testing the physical skills of my fellow prisoners as they developed and then declined with age. I also learnt computer programming without having direct access to a computer.

I will, in this chronicle, try and record my experiences as faithfully as possible and as far as my memory allows. The intention of this work is not to bemoan my treatment in prison except, perhaps, to draw attention to human rights abuses. I can frankly say that today I do not now bear any grudges against anybody. We were after all in a war situation and I often wonder what we would have done if our roles (warders and us) were reversed. Would our better education, our consciousness of oppression and appreciation of human rights and frailty have made any difference?

One of the more recent happenings that persuaded me to set my experiences in writing was my observation of the performance of a tour guide on Robben Island. I was flabbergasted to hear a member of the Robben Island Museum guides describe the Stone Quarry on Robben Island as "Madiba's Quarry" probably (in his mind) in competition with the 'van Riebeeck's quarry' opened by Jan van Riebeeck during the seventeenth century and still a scar on the Island. I knew that Mr. Mandela never worked at hard labour in that stone quarry and I would certainly not call a place of hardship and suffering after an honourable man who at that time was our state president. One would certainly not call an evil place like the gallows in Pretoria for example, after anybody. I also feel very uncomfortable when Museum Tour guides take their visitors to the Lime quarry to show where Mr. Mandela worked and pointing to the lime stone cliff that was obviously excavated by mechanical means. Mr. Mandela did work in the Lime Quarry at what was classified as 'suitable labour' in contrast to our hard labour in the stone quarry.

In this chronicle whenever I touch on events where I report differently from other writers I will try and document it with reference to Archival material.

In this narrative I will try to use the original Afrikaans words in the context where the event took place to give some flavour of the cultural milieu we lived in hoping it will not detract too much from the flow of the narrative. Afrikaans is a very colourful language and the Afrikaans of the Cape (where Afrikaans originated) even more so.

The other purpose of this text is really to put my experiences on paper for my grand children who may some day wonder what my experiences were, even if I do this with some hesitancy. A number of books have already been written describing experiences on Robben Island. Like this one, many recount personnel experiences. I must emphasize right from the beginning that I do not consider myself to be a politician. I try to be a scientist and find self-actualization in this activity. In this chronicle I will try to be as objective as possible but in an adverse life situation, errors of judgement and action are bound to occur. Even Nelson Mandela whose prison life was generally uneventful made errors. I will try and face my skeletons as best as I can and will let the reader be the judge.

Right from the start of my incarceration I made two resolutions. I strongly held the view that as a political prisoner one should continually plan to escape. I believed that the real work was outside prison and, further, to stop planning may be symptomatic of giving in to the effects of imprisonment and the abandonment of the cause that brought us to Robben Island in the first place. This is in contrast to the views of a number of politicians on Robben Island who felt that it was an 'honour' for them to be imprisoned and therefore, they said, one must surrender to the suffering and never try to escape. In support they would quote one of Nelson Mandela's speeches where he stated that he was prepared to die for the cause. This was then interpreted by these to imply that trying to escape was tantamount to an abandonment of this preparedness to die ideal (source: Robben Island Tour Guide, 2001). The second resolution that I undertook was to resist with all my being, the possible adverse effects of prison life since I suspected right from the start that there would be adverse effects – both physical and psychological.   I had yet to learn what these were.

I failed in both resolutions.   I never managed to escape despite numerous attempts and I will describe these in greater detail.   I also know that there must be after effects of my long term imprisonment, since right up to this day when ever I work in our garden at home with a spade or rake the songs of the hard labour gang in the stone quarry with which I once toiled still intrudes into my conscious.   I also know that I often lack spontaneous emotional warmth towards those dear to me. Also I still cannot sleep in clothes: whenever I try to sleep in pyjamas I wake up with a rising sense of unease and sometimes even panic.   This may be an after effect of my period in chains in the solitary cells of Robben Island, which coincided with the earthquake in the Cape.   This I will recount in greater detail at a later stage in this chronicle.   Textbooks I read stated that another of the effects of long-term imprisonment is a condition known as "chronophobia" which is the pathological fear of time.   I have not experienced this nor do I know any ex-prisoner who does.

I wish here to record my gratitude to Professor Charles Korr, Dr Helen Wright for their help as well as my wife and comrades for the encouragement to write this chronicle and to Achmad Casssiem who did the final language edit of the earlier version.

Chapter 1

The Prior years

I grew up in an area of Cape Town called 'Bo-Kaap'. I shared a room with two brothers in a three room Dutch styled house in Leeuwen Street. Our house was the only one in the area with a garden and fruit trees in the back yard.

My father, a businessman in the fish industry, was fairly wealthy. His father in turn was also in the fishing industry. My father died when I was six years old and my mother tried to take over as much of his business as possible. Unfortunately at that time it was not easy for a woman to function in a business world and her business deteriorated and then ultimately went bankrupt when debtors refused to honour their debts. I remember walking to some of the debtors to collect outstanding amounts and how some repudiated their debt. My eldest brother had to leave school after standard eight (the junior secondary level) to go and work in the building industry in order to help support the family. My mother tried her best to supplement the meagre family income by taking on embroidery work that she did during the nights under candle light so as to save on electricity. I was the second eldest in a family of four children and my mother struggled to give the rest of us a good education. She also tried her best to give us a normal childhood. She took us to our share of picnics, fun lands, parks, camps etc.

From the start Technology and Science was a constant source of fascination to me. During each end of year school vacation, starting from Primary School, I had a different project. First it was wood work and carpentry. I bought a chisel and a hammer but could not afford a plane. I had enough other tools to make wooden toys and a wooden fence round our back yard garden in Leeuwen Street. I also had an interest in gardening. With out knowing it, I constructed a type of Zen garden in the back of our house in Leeuwen Street and my sister and I would spend hours raking 'Zen' shapes and curves in the sand between the plants and the two trees that made up our garden. During heavy rains in winter the garden turned into a muddy pool fed by a broken gutter so then we would float handmade boats in the mud pool.

One year as a 'project' I set out to prepare laughing gas having read that it could instil laughter. For me it did not. I know because I did an experiment to prepare laughing gas or nitrous oxide by heating ammonium nitrate. I first had to wait for a convenient Sunday when there was no one else at home before I could heat the Ammonium nitrate as described in the Chemistry books. Unfortunately the round bottom flask I used to heat the ammonium nitrate in became loose from the clamp holding it over my mother's oil stove known as a primus. Perhaps the ammonium nitrate was really threatening to explode. As I learnt later Ammonium Nitrate is in fact an important ingredient of one of the easiest explosives to make. In my haste to save my only flask that I had bought at Scientific Suppliers in Pepper Street with great financial sacrifice, I grabbed the hot clamp, burnt my hand and somehow lost awareness of my environment because I later found myself lying on the kitchen floor and was not quite sure how I got there. This may be because I inhaled some of the gas that escaped into the air of the kitchen since Nitrous Oxide after all has anaesthetic properties or perhaps I lost consciousness because of the intense pain of my burnt hand. I was sorely disappointed since I experienced no laughter whatsoever. I felt more like crying. Fortunately nothing in the kitchen was damaged and I was quickly able to restore order.

Today ammonium nitrate is a classified explosive and cannot be bought over the counter and even the agricultural quality is controlled. During those years one could simply go to Scientific Suppliers in Pepper Street in Cape Town or Heyns and Matthews in Adderley Street and asked for a kilogram of ammonium nitrate and buy a supply of relatively pure salt without any questions. The agricultural quality could be obtained at the garden suppliers. Phenol, nitric acid, mercury, alcohol, potassium chlorate, sulphuric acid, glycerol (all the raw materials for explosives) were also then freely available over the same counter at Heyns Mathews in Adderley Street, Cape Town. Even toluene, the primary component of TNT, could be obtained if you placed an order. At Scientific Suppliers all types of laboratory apparatus could be bought without any questions asked. I later obtained round bottom flasks of various types and capacity, condensers, LPG Bunsen burners, funnels etc from there.

On another occasion I was interested in generating high voltage electricity and spent many hours after school and during the week-ends hand winding a Teslar coil. I obtained the circuit diagram from a Popular Electronics Journal. I was motivated by the anticipation of playing with a million volts of electricity at a million cycles per second. The device worked and was able to light up a fluorescent tube from a distance of a few centimetres or cause a dramatic stream of sparks from a ball of steel wool on the top of the coil. Unfortunately the coil did not work for too long. Perhaps a breakage developed somewhere along the kilometres of wire that made up the 60 cm coil. An old vacuum type valve drove the Teslar coil that I made. This pre-transistor device was not very reliable. Perhaps the valve just stopped functioning; I never had the chance to diagnose the problem. When I was arrested, the Security Police took the coil and energizer away for 'evidence'. I wonder what they thought it was. The circuit diagram was left behind and is still in my possession.

Another time, my interest was radio receivers and transmitters and I tried broadcasting but it often interfered with the local radio station. It was 'fun' seeing the Post Office or Police trucks coming up the street trying to pinpoint my transmitter. I also had less dangerous 'projects'. This included photography and motor mechanics. I learnt to recondition motor car engines by grinding and polishing valves, replacing piston rings. I took wedding photos as well as 8mm movie photography of the event. This latter was then rather expensive.

When I got to Standard 9 my interest turned to explosives. I spent hours in the State Library next to the Cape Town Botanical Gardens learning all about detonators, prima cords, electrical and chemical means of timing and setting off explosives. I already had some experience with Pyrotechnics since I always made my own fireworks during each annual celebration of Guy Fawkes Day. I knew how to colour the flame of fireworks, how to add bright sparkle using magnesium filings etc. I also had some experience with detonators having 'lifted' a supply from a government store along the Military Road on Signal Hill that we, as children, called the "Nuwe Pad" meaning New Road. I learnt the real danger of detonators when of one of my friends blew off a bit of his fingers holding a detonator in his hand as if it was a firecracker. I tried nitrating glycerol and I set this explosive off in the garden in the back of my mother's house using the domestic electricity supply to provide the spark that would trigger the explosion and using a suitable fuse to protect the circuit. I remember the excitement standing at the switch and doing the 'count down'. The explosion was deafening but did not draw much attention since I performed this experiment when everybody in Cape Town was setting off pyrotechnics for the annual Guy Fawkes festival that we in South Africa still celebrate having inherited the practice from Britain. Since I buried the charge in the soil the blast created a minor sandstorm blowing fine holes in the leaves of our apple tree. From books in the State Library in Queen Victoria Street I also learnt about offensive gasses such as that made from castor oil (ricin) and the chloro-acetophenones and how explosives can be used to carry and distribute these gasses. I later managed to get a supply of prima chord and detonators somewhere that I used for demonstrations to 'students' who wanted to learn about explosives.

I was, and still am, very fond of sweets and cakes. Perhaps this was one of the causes of my hyperactivity. I secretly used to sprinkle sugar on watermelons and sweet melons to enhance the taste. One day my mother made a bad purchase by buying a fairly unripe watermelon and I made the mistake of sprinkling sugar on it when she was not looking. She was intrigued to find a rather pink looking watermelon to be very sweet.

I was first made aware of oppression in South Africa by my grade two (it was then called substandard B) teacher. Mr. Martin came to our class at Prestwich Street Boy's School (PSB) to read to us from a newspaper about the Nationalist Government's new policy called 'apartheid' and he spelled it as 'aparthate' emphasizing the hate part of the term. Prestwich Street Boys' School had whites, blacks, Indians all in one class. When the nationalist government took over first the whites then the blacks disappeared from our classes. Mr. Martin predicted that hate would be the ultimate consequence of this new government policy. A succession of teachers then came over the years to try and teach us about

Democracy, Oppression, and the History of the Struggle against discrimination using the history of the French Revolution as a point of departure. We read about revolutions in other parts of the world and the story of Djamila Bopacha of the Algerian resistance against the French impressed us greatly. We also learnt about Che Guevara and Castro in South America and Mao in China. The history of the Russian revolution made fascinating reading. There were great teachers at Trafalgar High School like Slingers and Steenveldt and Cosmo Pieterse.

Pamphleteering as one of the earlier weapons of protest politics of the fifties was increasing. The aim was to increase awareness of our oppression and to announce to and invite people to Political Meetings and Rallies.   I was thirteen when I joined pamphleteering campaigns even though the then elders in the community viewed this with trepidation fearing tht the police will come and trample on the community. Later I attended meetings of the Anti CAD (i.e. Anti Coloured Affairs Department), the Teacher's League, and the Unity Movement etc. I also attended the occasional demonstration. The endless recounting to ourselves, at the various meetings, of how unfair the government was, only succeeded in instilling into me an increasing sense of helplessness and a need to do something practical. Perhaps these speeches were designed to do just this.

When the next phase of our struggle arrived, the phase of more active protest in the form of demonstrations using explosives, This change in mind set was driven particularly by killings at Sharpeville and elsewhere. I was ready. I was then studying chemistry at the university and explosives were, for some time, already my secret and favourite subject. The Political Organizations I knew then were mostly under the control and influence of intellectuals. They were content to continue discussing abstract topics. Lengthy discussions on subjects like the theory of oppression and the difference between 'horizontal' and 'vertical' oppression. These intellectuals were thus not really interested in demonstrations that involved any form of risk let alone armed struggles. It is not my intention here to minimize the contribution that these organizations made to the struggle. I believe that they kept hope alive and did much to educate us in politics.

My best friend's father was a tailor and he had a number of salesmen working for him. One of them serviced a black area called Langa in the Cape. I sneaked into the area and became acquainted with real oppression at first hand and discussions there in Langa were of a more practical and militant nature. There I met members of the Pan African Congress (PAC) who were discussing active revolution. Robert Sobukwe was the person and Nelson Mandela was still not too well known. This type of thinking was miles ahead of the organizations I knew. It was not easy to visit black areas during those years since a permit was needed on entry that also recorded the address of the person visited. We soon learnt to enter without bothering to register at the entry point but this carried some risk. The march to parliament, which had its roots in Langa, was organized by the PAC, made a very strong impression on me and so did the tragedy at Sharpeville.

At the Muslim Youth Movement (MYM) of which I was then a member I also met people who were interested in taking protest politics a little further. John Gomas from the communist party who was a regular visitor had the same idea.

George Allan Clarken came to Cape Town from Britain. He told us that he had previously served in the British Army and knew a lot about guns and was prepared to teach us what he knew. He became a Muslim, joined the Muslim Youth Movement (MYM) and boarded in Mr. Gool's carpenter's workshop next to the MYM premises in District Six. When George became Muslim he took on the name of Abdul Kareem. Becoming a Muslim made George a 'coloured' in terms of the then South African racial laws. A 'White' was defined as a person who looked obviously white and associated with whites. Becoming a Muslim implied that he had given up association with whites and would then be reclassified as 'coloured'. The nickname 'Al Prop" was added after he looked after a MYM fund raising bazaar Stall as 'proprietor' (the Al Prop). We acquired a .22 high power rifle and some handguns to practice with and Al Prop was the instructor. I, in turn, taught explosives and how to manufacture them. Al Prop at one stage wanted to know if it was possible to obtain chemicals or drugs that could be secreted in the city water supply that would make white people black. He had the rather amusing notion that if all people were black or blackened, apartheid policy would have had another problem to contend with. Out of curiosity I went through the literature that I could find in the State and Public Libraries and found that silver nitrate might be able to do the job if given in small doses over a longish period. The small doses were necessary because silver nitrate in larger doses causes diarrhoea. The problems were that the resultant skin colouration would be a bluish black and silver nitrate was fairly expensive. A number of people, including Mr. Gool had a deep suspicion of Al Prop as an enemy agent but the fact that he offered himself as a guinea pig and started taking silver nitrate to see if this could change the colour of white skins convinced me of Al Prop's good faith. There must be other medication that would cause better colouration since albinism is a condition that must have some better form of treatment.

Some of my earlier contributions to the life of our organizations included helping to smuggle and test unwrought gold to be used for the generation of funds. I never learnt where the gold came from but this was as it should be for obvious security reasons. My job was to determine the authenticity and purity of the gold. One afternoon returning with a gold nugget in my pocket to Abdul Kareem's lodging, I found people there who looked like the police. Al Prop saw me coming and he glared at the onlookers and shouted to them to clear off in rather rude language since his arrest was not their business. These sharp insults flung to no one in particular by the otherwise mild mannered Abdul Kareem definitely identified the police for me and indicated that I had get out of the area as quickly as possible or also risk getting arrested. Al Prop was arrested and taken to Roland Street Jail. After that we had the problem of getting him out of prison before the gold division connected him with political matters and informed the Security Police. How he was sprung from prison I never found out. I saw it as my task to help get him out of the city and if possible the country.

A car was 'donated' for the purpose but, for security reasons, there was a restriction on how long the car could be available to protect the owner should we be caught. We were given four days (over a week end) to use the 'borrowed' car. After that the car would be reported 'stolen'. Abdul Kareem did most of the driving up to the border. Near Francis Town, but on the South African side, Abdul Kareem got out and walked down the road and crossed the border into Botswana at a point just off the main highway a few metres from the border post. He arrived safely since he later sent for his sleeping bag. I never saw him again and I still have his photograph and that of his sister. I later read about him been with the African National Congress and another time hunting crocodiles, but this was never corroborated.

One of the most ardent political activists I knew was Achmad Cassiem. I came to know him through his father Boeta Cassiem of the MYM who taught Arabic and Islamic Law. I later saw Achmad at Trafalgar High School when I became a new science teacher there. Achmad was then a Matriculation student. We became friends but I never taught any of the classes he attended. Achmad was (and still is) keenly interested in practical politics. These issues are the topics of another chronicle and will therefore not be recounted here.

My main interest then was learning about and teaching the making and use of explosives (which we called 'cosmetics'). My lectures, often to a rather loose group of political activists, included an exposition of the properties and mechanisms of action of explosives, how to trigger them by electrical or chemical means and how delay fuses (both chemical and electrical) work and the difference between propellants and true explosives. We also dealt with how easily obtainable substances such as pool chlorine and fertilizer can be used to construct bombs

I was also interested in how explosives could be used to disperse offensive or strategic gasses that may be useful in our struggle, particularly gasses which would not cause permanent harm since our own people may be in the vicinity.

There was one particular practical demonstration I will never forget. This took place in somebody's storage garage in District Six. One evening I was demonstrating how to join prima chord to detonator caps when I looked up to see one of the 'students' having joined the chord and crimped it correctly into the detonator cap putting a match to the chord. He told us not to worry; he would simply clip the flame off with a cutter just before it reached the detonator. Unfortunately the cutter was stiff and he could not clip the flame off. The flame passed the point where he intended to make the cut and he had to struggle to open the cutter to attempt a further clipping off of the flame. We could not escape from the garage because it was locked with a padlock from the outside for security reasons and the window was stuck with age so that the detonator could not be thrown out of the window in time. The cap, in any case, looked so small that nobody was actually too worried yet nobody wanted to pull the cord out of the cap since at the introduction of the lecture I recounted how a detonator cap blew of the fingers of a childhood friend.. The cap exploded with a deafening noise amplified by the confines of our 'demonstration room'. It was there that I first observed the phases of shock reaction I later read about in psychology textbooks whilst studying at URI (the 'University of Robben Island')). I saw 'students' in that garage, who could not get beyond the 'recall' phase of the shock reaction, walking up and down the garage each repeating his own favourite exclamation. It took some time for everybody to settle down again and when I later met some of those students the recall of this event was one of their first topics of conversation. Some actually thought that they narrowly escaped being blown up and frequently talked about their 'near death experience'.

Chapter 2

Arrest

One evening on the way home after testing the explosive and dispersal properties of picric acid on the Strandfontein beach, a very isolated area outside Cape Town, Achmad suggested that we use the last sample on a suitable Electricity sub-station on our way back. We (I, Achmad Cassiem, and Marnie Abrahams) were caught by the vigilant police as we cruised along De Waal Drive. We must have been watched. We never had the chance to investigate this possibility and I still wonder about this. I do, however, have an hypothesis. I was then friendly with a white girl and this may have contributed to the risk of police surveillance. There was on the statutes of South African law an act known as the South African 'Immorality' act. This law made it a serious 'criminal' offence for people from different racial groups to associate in with one another on a social level especially if they were of the opposite sex. It was far more serious than the "reckless eye balling" in America where it was an offence for a black person to look at a white woman. This offence, under the Apartheid government carried a prison sentence of seven years for both, if found guilty and thus far more serious than the crime of 'reckless eye balling' in the American Southern States. The police were particularly watchful of this 'crime' and a division of police (called the Immorality Squad) was especially set up and tasked to watch out, investigate and arrest suspects contravening this law. The other hypothesis was that the police knew about my involvement with Al Prop and his disappearance.

We were then roughly pushed at gunpoint into the police van and taken to Woodstock Police Station. Belts, watches, pens, guns and money were taken away and we were booked in and thrown into separate cells.

The following morning we were transferred by armed police escort vans to the Cape Town Police Headquarters at Caledon Square to be handed over the Security Police. We were now placed in detention without trial as terrorists / saboteurs and the only requirement was to be so certified by any senior police officer. That was all the law then required to be detained without trial. Section 29 of this same law specifically stated that such prisoners would have no access to lawyers. Each prisoner was allocated to a small dirty cell on the first floor at the Police Headquarters at Caledon Square barely one metre wide and just over two metres long painted a drab grey.

Left to myself I inspected my new accommodation. In the corner on one wall was a rather good pencil sketch of a naked woman. On the other wall were crude letterings which urged the reader to "kill all the bastards" followed by the announcement that the "Mongrel was here". I could not help wondering just who was to be killed - perhaps the arrogant and all powerful security police. The door to the cell was thick wood with a covering of metal also painted a drab grey. Before being pushed into the cell I noticed the door had a large padlock outside to supplement a mortise lock as if some treasure was normally kept in these rooms. At about three quarters the height of the door was a hole with a cover slip on the outside. I peeped through this hole and could shift the cover using a stubby pencil I had in my back pocket but saw only the wall opposite. Below the door was a gap that allowed air in. I later found that often the same air draught could become fresh and cold, which the dirty blanket could not protect against. At the further end of the cell opposite the door and at about one and a half metres from the floor was a window covered with a dirty heavy closed meshed wire grating, a few bars on the inner side of the grating and no glass. I jumped up grabbed the bars and pulled myself up to peer through the window but could see nothing of the street below although the sound of traffic and voices could faintly be heard from somewhere outside the window.

On the floor of the cell were a soiled mattress and a lumpy cushion with two smelly blankets as bedding. I was to discover the lice later. There was no toilet or water supply in that cell. The floor itself was polished cement and in the centre of the concrete ceiling fairly high up was a bulb covered with thick wired glass providing a low level yellowish glare twenty four hours a day. I exercised a bit by running on the spot, did a few push-ups and then sat down on the mattress to contemplate my predicament. I thought of all that was still to be done to promote the revolution and my intense desire to be part of the action only lead to a sense of frustration. I worked hard to suppress the anxiety and sense of helplessness created by the situation. I also thought of my mother, worrying, when I did not return home that night. She must have waited up all night for me as she usually did when I came home late and the anxiety she must have suffered made me sad.

After ten o'clock the following morning (as signalled by the nearby city hall bell) the Security Police came to fetch me for my first dose of unpleasantness in the form of threats, physical persuasions and sleep deprivation served up by Spyker van Wyk and his cronies, who I now know many of my predecessors had already encountered. I thus underwent the same experience that many others in the same situation in South Africa went through during that period, the same experience of trauma, batons, arms twists, the same sense of anxiety compounded by uncertainty and the same guilt for leaving one's family. The same backward shove across a desk with one of them inducing a severe stomach-ache with the aid of a rubber baton across the stomach. Rubber truncheons can be extremely painful when applied across the victim's abdomen without causing much externally visible signs of injury. The intention, I believe, is to cause internal injuries and prolonged suffering. After this treatment they would take perverse pleasure in pushing you backwards across a desk just to observe your reflexive fear response. A chalk circle was drawn also and you, the victim, had to remain standing in it or else 'get fixed up'. I understood fixed up meant beaten up or, as they colourfully put it, 'dondered' and 'bliksemmed' (both Afrikaans metaphors for extremely heavy weather conditions that would be directed to you the victim using their fists, batons or other similar tools).   My first encounter left me with severe stomach-ache possibly caused by the resultant internal injury from the rubber baton treatment.   Nobody I know who went through these experiences freely talks about it. I certainly never could. I was sorely tempted to delete this.

At the second encounter with these thugs my biggest problem was the fear of again being pushed backwards across the desk for the rubber baton treatment but this time the start was gentler. I was told to again stand in the chalk circle drawn in the centre of the room. I noticed that the desk was pushed to the wall to accommodate this new foolery.

Standing inside the chalk circle appeared to me to be rather stupid since I thought I would able to stand there for days on end looking at their ugly faces. Standing in that circle it seemed I only had to listen to the threats of getting shot or hanged or how I was going to break stones for the rest of my life in the quarries of

Robben Island. There on Robben Island I would freeze my ass off or burn black in the blazing sun with only hard stale bread for food and bitter brack water to drink. Thinking back I thought that it was funny that those security policemen did not know that the fare was not dry bread and water there in the punishment section of Robben Island but maze 'rice' water and nothing else. Bread there, even stale bread, was a luxury food item.

I am not certain how long this sleep deprivation episode went on since I had no watch and daylight was not visible in that room, but to me it seemed to have gone on for days since a succession of policemen came to relieve one another throughout the period. Gradually fatigue set in and a pain started in the arches of my feet and in my knees that I tried to alleviate by flexing my feet and knees and standing on tiptoe, which seemed to amuse my tormentors. I remember gradually getting dizzy. In fact I am not sure when the dizziness started. After some time flashes of bright colours appeared in my visual field that seemed to rise from the floor and float to the ceiling. I could not help gazing with some fascination at these mirages. The flashes became more frequent, then lost colour and became bright white and black zigzag patterns visible even when I closed my eyes. The voices of my tormentors became softer and seemed to be coming from an ever-increasing distance. I vaguely heard them first talking about some rugby match and then I heard then shouting at somebody to wake up. When I opened my eyes there appeared gaps in my visual field since I could see van Wyk's mouth and not the rest of his face and I could not see Ginis' ears but I could make out his eyes. A headache crept up from my neck and it later felt as if there was something loose in my head judging from the pain and sounds I heard when I moved my head. The dull ache behind my eyes was also getting more intense. A weird and unsettling sense of unreality took over my consciousness – a strange feeling of an altered mental state as if my body and my mind had become separate entities. I frequently closed my eyes and would then be shaken and smacked and punched awake but this did not cause me any pain. I was told that if I did not wake up electrical assistance would be used to keep me awake and then I would 'bars' (the Afrikaans for burst). I was now getting beyond caring and despite the dazed state, I developed a faint curiosity about what electrical assistance they were talking about. After this my systems just shut down. I do not remember what happened after wards.

When I regained consciousness I found myself been hustled down and then up the steps to the cells. Perhaps they saw that I lost interest and awareness of the surroundings and stopped paying attention to them. A 'coloured' and 'white' policeman stood waiting for me and helped me up the last of the steps and back to my quarters. I was pushed or rather thrown into the cell, hit the wall on the opposite side and collapsed on the mattress. Despite the fatigue I could at first not sleep because of the severe headache, the pains in my jaw, the nausea, the disturbing light patterns and the unusual level of tension. I had a vague panic attack that I was going blind and that I was dying. It took some effort to suppress this. I had some blood in my nose and my lower lip felt thick and my upper lip seemed split and I sat wondering what had caused these injuries. I also felt a bump on my head but this was not painful. Perhaps this was all the remnants of the persuasions to keep awake. It was a relief to lie down. Even the soles of my feet hurt. My body still felt as if it did not belong to me but the returning pains certainly did. Eventually I did not fall asleep but simply lost consciousness. I recovered feeling stiff and the aches seemed to have spread to all parts of my body. My vision seemed to have improved though. I again tried to sleep.

Fleas or lice were the next problem. This made continuous sleep difficult. It seemed I first had to catch every flea and louse in the bedding. The lice were greyish white in colour and I could not suppress an odd racial thought. I again took stock of my injuries and catalogued a sore eye, a bump on my head and a loose tooth and felt grateful to come out of that episode with so little injury. I still have the scar on my upper lip (now covered with a moustache) to remind me of those days with van Wyk, Ginnis and company. On the other hand I have heard of others who came out with missing fingernails having had them non-surgically removed and of still others who died supposedly having fallen down the stairs or jumped through the window. I then remembered thinking with anxiety that this might be just the beginning and things may in fact be far from over.

The visual disturbance and headaches subsided but came back at unpredictable intervals during that period and even later on the Island. I still have, even now, about one or two episodes a year of visual disturbance with flashes of light and a strange sense of disorientation but fortunately it never lasts for more that an hour.

After few days respite the 2.00am interrogations began again; first on a daily then a random basis all arranged by Ginis, Spyker van Wyk and his pals with the same old demands that I tell them everything and name everybody who was involved. Everybody else, they said, had already told them everything. It struck me as odd that they then still needed that information from me.

Some white members of the African Resistance Movement (ARM) were detained at the same time and their families kept careful check on their physical well being using their lawyers and contacts in high places. This, I believed, saved me from the more physical forms of torture at the hands of the security police who sometimes took out their electric shock machine and their wet bags used to simulate drowning, pliers and rubber batons to intimidate me.

I one day also found myself at the butt of another of the security police's perverse fun when they told me that they had decided to release me and that I was free to go. I remembered the relief and jubilation as I walked down the passage to the door willing myself not to loose dignity and run. At the door I was met my van Wyk who told me that he was re-arresting me on the charge of sabotage and he lifted his jacket to show me his gun. I supposed just in case I decided to make a dash for it. He then seemed to take great pleasure in observing the deflation when marching me back to my cell on the first floor and the rounds of the nightly questions started all over again.

I did tell the police that I had an interest in explosives and I had manufactured it for experimental purposes. I could hardly deny this since my hands were stained a bright yellow by the explosive called tri-nitrophenol. Because of this our lawyers thought it wise for me not to go to the witness box when our trial finally came up. I do not think it would have mattered.

Detention without trial is designed to disorientate the detainee and the transition from an active life to the passive existence in solitary confinement interspersed with violence, the threat of violence and sleep deprivation was rather difficult. The uncertainty, the fear and the absolute power the security police had over the prisoner was very disconcerting. It seems as if they could injure, maim or kill with total impunity. The more immediate problem during the early days of confinement was, also, the freezing wind that rushed in under the door of the cell.

We were allowed 15 minutes of exercise per day (which included time for washing and toilet). Exercise meant walking around a circle under a barbed wire 'ceiling' through which a square of blue sky was visible. Even during this stage, as I walked round that little quad on the first floor at Caledon Square, I was looking for opportunities to escape. This was difficult since every cell door had to be opened with two keys each handled by different policemen and only one prisoner was let out at a time. This meant that two policemen had to be present before a cell door could be opened. It struck me that this was really how one safe guarded something in a bank and this somehow made me feel less of a person.

On the first floor at Caledon Square with me were Achmad Cassiem, Solly Keraan, James Marsh, Manie Abrahams and Eddy Daniels. Solly was arrested later. Spike de Keller and the other 'white' detainees were held on a different floor as required by the apartheid laws but we could hear them shouting to one another. Alex later joined us. Alex was then, or perhaps later, recruited to become a state witness against us but we were then not aware of this and we naively spoke to one another about what happened. We were thus dismayed when he appeared in court sitting in the witness box telling the court what we spoke about in the police cells and how he recognized my voice. However, this speeded up the police investigations and perhaps saved us from further torture and injury. They also tried to force Ollie Keraan to become a witness but he bluntly refused, so out of revenge they served him with a banning order for five years after we were transported to Robben Island.

At that time the film "To Kill a Mocking Bird" was on the film circuit but shown at cinemas for whites only. It was the story of a black defended by a white lawyer in a criminal case and thus not regarded as suitable for viewing by blacks. I wanted to go and see the film and wrote a note to remind myself since it was possible for me to slip into a white cinema after a white friend bought the tickets. The Security Police found the note and took it completely out of context. Now they wanted to know who the mocking bird was that we were going to kill. I told them that it was a film but they did not believe me since that film was reserved for viewing exclusively by whites. They thought that the mocking bird was one of their coloured politician stooges and I spent many hours of pain and lost sleep trying to explain to them that it was not true. This note was used in court to demonstrate what the lawyers called mense rea or 'evil intent'. They said that I had killing and murder on my mind.

Occasionally the two-policemen rule at the cell door at Caledon Square was broken and one policeman came who handled both keys to our cells and, in order to save time, he even opened two cells at a time. This must have occurred on the occasions when the police were on short staff during public holidays. The escape plan we cooked up was simple. When this policeman was on and both Eddy and I were out we would overpower him, take the keys, let everyone else out and see how best we could get out of the building and the city. Unfortunately the careless policeman was not a regular on our floor and we waited in vain for him to come on duty. I think the mere planning to escape had some positive, albeit small, effect on our morale.

A magistrate came to visit us occasionally even though the regulations said 'regularly'. The cell door was then thrown open without warning, the magistrate would hurriedly asked 'are you all right' and then the door quickly closed and the magistrate would rush off before anything could be said to him. On one particular occasion I heard the magistrate go to Eddie and when he came to me next I was ready with my complaint. I hurriedly told him that the cells were cold and that we needed heaters. He just laughed and told me that this was not a holiday resort and that we were suspected of having committed serious crimes against the security of the state. We did, however, get additional blankets one of which I could use as a draught block for my door.

Food was sent to us regularly from our respective homes. This replaced the jam and bread three times a day the police offered their prisoners. I later learnt that the menu offered depended on the colour of the skin of the prisoner. White detainees had better food and blacks were given food of poorer quality. We protested against this and were then provided with food from the Police Mess on instructions of a colonel McIntyre to the chagrin of the Security Police. The food parcels from home were always carefully searched. Sandwiches or pies were opened but to our surprise the messages that Esme, one of the senior students at Trafalgar High School who cared for and supported us in many ways, placed inside the coffee flask was passed on without being opened. Perhaps the police knew about this and were fishing for further information.

To relieve the monotony and tension we had 'concerts' where Achmad and Alex featured as singers from within the confines of their respective cells. Alex was a good singer with a rich tenor and his repertoire varied from light opera to popular songs. From his cell he sang the "Drinking Song", the "Ava Maria" with a voice like Mario Lanza, or "Another Sleepless Night" or "The Evergreen Tree" from the album of Pat Boone. Achmad sang the then popular and very fitting Elvis Presley song 'I want to be free' or "I have been judged convicted and condemned" a song actually about a lover whose girl suspected him of infidelity and gave him a walking ticket without a 'hearing' and the song accused her of been the judge and jury all in one. At six o'clock on Sunday evenings the nearby city hall bells gave us a concert for about an hour. Classical pieces from the operas were then chimed out.

Occasionally, under pressure from us, shouting demands from our respective cells, Eddy would sing his favourite song. It was about a randy tinker with his "kidney wiper" and his "jolly old balls of steel hanging way beyond his heels". The song ended when the tinker died and went to hell and what this ultra randy tinker did to the devil there with his jolly old balls of steel. Eddy's other song was 'Galway bay". The irony was that when we reached Robben Island we found the common law prisoners also sang the same song but with wording changed to " have you ever been across the sea to Robben Island" and something about seeing prisoners in the quarry making clay.

James entertained us with contortion exercises by calling out physical exercises with limb positions we should try. I always though he was making these impossible limb positions up but I later saw that he could actually put his toe in his mouth. Others had jokes to tell and riddles to pose. The one I remember was the names of various Chinese authors to fit the situation – like who wrote the book "Floods over China". The answer would be 'Wan Long Pee or the book 'Spots on the Wall' by Wu Flung Dung.

One day a criminal was brought to our floor there at the Police Head Quarters at Caledon Square. Perhaps the cells on the lower floor were full. After the policemen left, everyone tried to call to him in order to get some news. I was nearest and managed to get my voice through to his cell. I asked him (in Afrikaans) what he was here for and he told me that he was charged with murder, rape and attempted murder and he then asked me why I was arrested (caught as he put it). I told him that we were all here for politics. After a brief and very pregnant silence, possibly, to digest that type of information, his amazed response was "But that is dangerous!" This brought home to us how the general prison population viewed political activity. He could unfortunately not give us any useful information except advice. His main advice to us was not to give the white man (boere) any slack (draad he called it). This advice was, nevertheless, a bit heartening.

My brother and Boeta Salie, Solly Keraan's father, discovered the location of our cells and one day came to the side street to talk to us from the outside. I could not see them since the cell had bars and a close meshed grating on the outside but I recognized their voices. They assured us that everything at home was all right and that they were getting Mr. Dullah Omar (a Lawyer) and Mr. Kies (an advocate) to take up our defense. Mr. Omar would come and visit us as soon as we were released from detention without trial and formally charged. An organization based in Britain known as "Defense and Aid" would pay all our legal cost. Unfortunately the police heard us talking and rushed out to arrest both my brother and Mr. Keraan. They were brought in to spend the weekend in jail but on a floor below us. We heard that one pleaded guilty and the other one not guilty in order to minimized the effect. The guilty one had to pay a R10 fine for 'communicating with prisoners'. It could have been much worse. South Africa was after all, a police state then.

A date for our court case was finally set and we were released from detention to become 'awaiting trial prisoners'. Copies of a Charge Sheet also called an Indictment were handed to us and we were taken to Pollsmoor Prison a few kilometres outside Cape Town and put into one cell. The cell at Pollsmoor was big enough to house at lease fifty prisoners and I felt a bit strange in such a large environment after the confines of the detention without trial accommodation. It had a toilet and shower facilities that were luxurious compared to Caledon Square. We then had the first visit from Dallah Omar who was appointed as our lawyer. Eddy Daniels from the African Resistant Movement joined us in this large communal holding cell at Pollsmoor Prison. Escape now became a possibility and we immediately set about planning this and we let Esme know of our plans via the coffee flask postal system she set up for us. Eddy managed with promises of payments, to get a warder Arthur McDillon to smuggle a hacksaw blade in to us and to take messages to Esme and others to arrange a get away car for us. Esme approached a local political organization for help that took up the matter in a lengthy debate. The local electricity supply sub station also had to be incapacitated so that we could slip away in the dark. McDillon brought us the required hack saw blades and we proceeded to cut through the bars of the cell, singing to drown the sound of the hacksaw whilst waiting for the organization to come to a decision. I cannot sing to save my life and was thus saddled with most of the sawing, sharing the effort with Achmad and Eddy. Mr. Dallah Omar came to visit us and when we whispered to him that we were busy cutting the bars to our cell he was totally flabbergasted. When he found his tongue he reminded us that we were enemies of the state and the police would not think twice before shooting us if they got the opportunity to do so.

Dallah continued to be our lawyer and I am sure had it been somebody else they would have dropped out immediately. Dallah was already getting a reputation as a political lawyer. The irony is that with the first democratically elected government in post apartheid South Africa Dallah became the Minister of Justice.

We eventually cut through the bars but had to wait until transport could be arranged, which we learnt would be delayed once more. The biggest problem was disabling the electricity sub station supplying power to Pollsmoor Prison.   Achmad, the artist amongst us, managed to put the segment of the bar that we cut out back and to 'fix' or camouflage the cuts in the bars with putty and some oil paint mixed to match the colour of the bars that came in with the artist set he asked for.   It seems that warder Arthur McDillon, who Indris Naidoo in his book called 'Warder A', was making roaring business deals by selling hacksaw blades to many of the sentenced common law prisoners as well us. Some of them were caught. Perhaps an informer from among the common law prisoners went to the prison authorities to, using prison idiom, pimp on them. Unfortunately some criminals in an adjacent cell saw us talking to McDillon and they informed the warders so that unknowingly we too came under suspicion. McDillon was later arrested and sentenced to three years imprisonment for this as well as for smuggling Hacksaw blades to us.

That evening we had our first demonstration of prison warder as opposed to police brutality. We heard shouting and screaming and peeping out we saw a row of prisoners naked and chained been chased and assaulted in the passage by about twenty warders using batons, rubber truncheons and long sprightly canes. We later learnt that their crime was that they attempted to escape and that part of their punishment was the chains and the free for all assault termed 'a carry-on'. A 'carry on' is where the Head of the Prison instructs the warders to carry on and freely assault prisoners chained together with batons, sticks, canes or fists or any other implement.   Prisoners feared this carry on since it generally lead to bleeding heads, bruised bodies split skins and deep raw weals that needed medical attention. It struck me as strange hearing Afrikaans speaking warders use this English term.   They must have learnt this from the British during the colonial period.

The following day we were visited by a group of warders together with the Head of the Prison wielding batons and canes in a very intimidating manner. We were ordered to strip naked and all our clothing and belongings thoroughly searched and we thought that the carry on will now be visited onto us. Fortunately, McDillon had already taken the hacksaw blades away. The efforts every one of us made not to look up at the bars just to check if the quality of the camouflage was still OK were almost tangible. They found nothing on us and we had a tense moment when one warder, in obvious frustration, made a swipe at some of the window bars with his baton. Fortunately he stopped and they left us. We could not believe our luck. The next day was spent anxiously waiting for news about the car we asked for and the arrangements that had been made to disable the electricity sub station so that we could slip away in the dark. Later that day the search party came back accompanied by the security police. This time we were marched off to another cell and we then heard a rhythmic tapping sound as each bar was tested with a baton. The tapping sound came to an abrupt halt followed immediately by a ringing sound as the cut out bars struck the cement floor. That sound seemed to reach down into the very bottom of my stomach. The contingent of warders and police came to fetch us. We were marched with great hurry back to our cell to confront the Head of the Prison who stood wordlessly pointing his swagger stick to the gap in the bars reminding me of the statue of Cecil John Rhodes in the Cape Town Botanical Gardens pointing to his 'hinterland". We all tried our best to look suitably surprised at the gap and Eddy tried to explain to the chief warder that we could not really be held responsible for any defects that may be in the bars of Polsmoor Prison. The Chief Warder and his men seemed to have some difficulty trying to contain themselves and the Chief Warder then spoke something about fairies in the night that must have caused the bars to break.

During that period we went to the Supreme Court every day to have our case heard and assault marks would have had to be explained (or so we thought). Shortly after that more security policemen arrived and they bundled us into a van and drove in a convoy straight back to Caledon Square and back to our old five star single cell accommodation on the first floor at the Police

Headquarters in Cape Town. The old regimen of exercise once a day, doors opened by two warders for one prisoner at a time for a walk in the little courtyard with its layer of barbed wire covering the sky became the order of the day once more. Round and around the circle under the barbed wired sky I again walked for fifteen minutes a day during week ends, a quick visit to the toilet and back to the one by two cells again became the routine that we had learnt during detention without trial period. This was broken by glorious outings to the Supreme Court to attend our trial. The trial often seemed to have nothing to do with us. The discussion at one stage was about what constituted premises like buildings, fields etc. If two people were on the same premises and one person had explosives then the learned lawyers said the other may be called an accomplice if he knew the former had an explosive purely by virtue of being on the same premises. The 'learned' court decided that a road is also premises and if two people were a thousand kilometres away on the same road (premises) and one knew the other had an explosive then they, by this definition, could be called accomplices and could be charged as such. There were explosives in the car I was driving and therefore everybody in the car was an accomplice of mine even though we may not have been 'of common mind' which our defence advocates argued was a requirement for one to be called an accomplice of the other. I was not quite sure if the term 'learned' was used in irony.

Out of boredom Achmad drew the court scene with the cocky prosecutor (Mr. Lategan) as a rooster and the predator like judge as a scrawny eagle with his gaily coloured robe sitting high up on his bench with his two assessors – one with prominent cauliflower ears, which made me wonder what a boxer was doing sitting next to the judge. Mr. Kies, our advocate, told us that the two assessors were magistrates and they replaced a jury in political cases such as ours. Men accused of common law or criminal offences at that time could still opt for a jury instead of assessors.

I did not take the witness stand and the smug looking judge later accused our defence of 'playing hide and seek with the facts'. My brother was called to identify my handwriting and he pretended not to be able to give a clear identification. The 'learned' judge in summing up declared that if a brother does not expressly state that the handwriting in question was not his sibling's then this expression of doubt can be regarded as a positive identification.

After about a month the court hearing came to a close and we were duly pronounced 'guilty'. The day before the sentence was to be read out our families wanted to know what we would like for our last meal before the prison sentences started. We asked for chicken curry. Chicken curry always reminds me of that last meal before going off to Robben Island.

After listening to a lecture from the smug looking judge in his bright red robe about my irresponsibility as a teacher misleading innocent students, I was told that I would be sentenced to twelve years in prison. I found the bit about innocent students ironical since I knew that politics had taken root at Trafalgar High School even before my arrival there. I must have smiled a little at this thought because at our appeal at the Appellate Division mention was made of the fact that I was not shocked at the sentence so that led to the inference was that I too must have considered it adequate. I was amused to hear that this factor was taken into consideration when the Appellate Division in Bloemfontein considered if the sentence should be reduced.

We were then handcuffed and taken down via a tunnel to the holding cells at the bottom of the Supreme Court. I briefly looked at some writing on the wall of the cell made by a previous convict who claimed to be innocent that read "six jeres, six laatjies and innersent" and I thought of my own twelve 'jeres' (years). I then did not know what the 'laatjies' was. I later discovered it was lashes awarded for violent crimes and rapes and the defendant with his six jeres and laaties may very well have been a rapist. In another corner was a notice proclaiming that "Killer was here". This made me feel truly caught up in the South African 'judicial' and criminal system. We were then hustled out of the cell to the loading zone.

My family came and said a tearful goodbye to us standing behind the gate on the side of the court facing the street, waiting for the truck to take us to the dock where a boat would take us to Robben Island. I felt a bit bad because my family looked to me as an income resource to help get the family out of its financial stagnation. All my mother's sisters were able to move out into better houses as their children became economically active and there was I on my way to Robben Island.

I had read the newspaper descriptions by ANC and PAC prisoners of the cruel and harsh conditions on Robben Island but this did not worry me unduly. I was so optimistic about the revolution that was starting a new phase that the sentence did not trouble me at all. Besides, I also had escape plans in mind since I wanted to remain involved in the revolution.

After our families were told to leave we were fitted with two sets of handcuffs and two sets of leg irons. The double sets were apparently a precaution against a possible escape attempt since we now had a record. Chained together in pairs we hobbled onto a prison truck surrounded by police escorts armed with Belgium FN rifles. We had to help one another up the steps to the bed of the truck. The door of the truck was slammed shut and locked. On the road to the docks I peeped out of the prison truck for one last nostalgic look at Cape Town and noticed the late afternoon sunshine and the newspaper posters advertising my sentence in big bold letters. Our truck and convoy of escorting cars with guns sticking out of the windows arrived at East Pier, the then gateway to Robben Island Prison. I smelled for a last time the free odour of fish from the boats in the vicinity. The convoy was deployed with military precision and each guard armed with an automatic rifle took up a strategic post around the dock area. We were told to get off the truck and shuffled aboard the Diaz and unceremoniously pushed down into the goods hold. A coil of old rope broke my fall. The rope tying the boat to the quay was cast off and we chugged out of the docks to the open sea. Warders and their children came to look down at us awkwardly lying chained together in the hold and I heard one warder explaining to the children that we were terrorists and enemies of their country who wanted to kill South Africans as if we were not also South Africans, although perhaps of a different colour but definitely of a different privilege level. I will always remember that sea sick filled trip to Robben Island with the nauseating smell of diesel fumes and rotten fish. I am not normally prone to seasickness but the uncertainty must have contributed to my mal ease. We were further continuously reminded by the police and the warders, who taunted us from the opening above, that we were meant for 'Devils Island' where we would be 'crying bitter tears' and I wondered if they were some of the devils or were there special beings who were devils there on the Island we were heading towards. We were promised lots of 'carry-ons' with rubber batons and pick axe handles and we would have 'rice water' for food and hard labour in the quarry where we would sweat our guts out in the summer and freeze our butts off in the winter. A warder by the name of Botma was in charge on Robben Island and he knows exactly what to do with terrorists and Poqos like us. Poqo was the military wing of the PAC and I later learnt that all political prisoners were called 'Poqos". We would be released, if we managed to survive, when we were old and broken from the life of hardship on Devil's Island. The idea of fighting the government was stupid and would only bring destruction and death to those who dare to do so, as we would be experiencing soon.

That boat trip to Robben Island seemed never ending.

Twelve years seemed so long that I surmised that when I returned to Cape Town (if ever) then cars could be flying and people would be living on the moon and come to visit earth during the weekends.   Most of man's illnesses would be cured.   I remembered vacillating between optimism and pessimism.

Life for me was then changing. I had a sense of an unknown and difficult chapter in my life opening and that I would need great strength to see it through.   I also knew that I had to adapt as quickly as possible. What made it even more unsettling was that there appeared to be no end to the chapter now opening up. Then again I experienced the only positive emotion, which was the relief of getting out of the clutches of the Security Police and I thought conditions could not be as bad on Robben Island as the dingy police cells with brutish sadists as personnel with their rubber batons, chalk circles and electricity machines.

Chapter 3

Devils Island

About an hour later and with us feeling green with seasickness aggravated by the uncertainty and apprehension, the boat docked at the Robben Island harbour. We were told to "kruip uit " (crawl out) of the hold. On 'surfacing' and having steadied myself as best as I could, I noticed the name of the harbour was Murray's Harbour and I wondered who Murray was. Still in handcuffs and leg irons we hobbled from the boat to an awaiting truck and were driven at great speed to the gate of the Ultra Maximum Security Prison of Robben Island. As we arrived I noticed a huge motor driven siren mounted on top of the roof and I imagined the noise should it go off to signal an escape. A siren of that size could easily be audible as far as Cape Town. Cape Town at that stage seemed to be to be very far away indeed. The prison was a partially constructed building made of blue slate stone with solid blue slate stone steps leading to a steel gate painted a dull blue grey colour. There were rooms on both sides of the gate. At each window were massive four centimetre thick bars. I had to remind myself not to call the subdivisions of the Prison building rooms but rather cells. After my release thirteen years later I had to remind myself not to call the rooms in my mother's house 'cells' nor to refer to the wards of the hospital where I later worked as cells. I looked with a sense of dismay at the sinister grey stone building and I thought that if the revolution did not take off then this could very well be my home for the next twelve years at least. The word 'home' had a very incongruous sound. I was promptly shaken out of this reverie by the carriage of the truck starting to tip and we were deposited with arms and legs entangled in a bundle on the ground in front of the prison, our first lesson that from now onwards we are to be considered as things and not human.

We struggled to get up. I looked again at the bars and wondered how easy it would be to saw through. The bars at the windows looked more like tubes that, I thought, should be fairly easy to cut with a good hacksaw. The problem would be where can one find hacksaws blades in a place like this with such angry warders crawling all over the place. To try to escape was, nevertheless, definitely on my mind and I thought that I must start collecting as much information about the prison and its security measures as possible.

A warder, one from the convoy who escorted us, stepped up the blue stone steps to the steel front gate, stamped his feet on the steps, grabbed and banged the huge brass knocker attached to the gate and shouted "Dankie Hek" (Thank you the gate). A warder appeared and he had with him the largest key I ever saw. This he jammed into an equally large black lock and opened the gate with a noisy clatter. A small key and lock would have fitted the purpose adequately and I wondered if the key has been made big just for effect. I couldn't then help thinking of a Bo-Kaap idiom "… a bek soos 'n tronkslot" (mouth like a prison lock) describing a person who can keep a secret. We were hurried through two gates; the one gate was closed before the other one opened and arrived at the reception where the two sets of leg irons and the handcuffs were removed. It seemed that we arrived safely and in one piece. The warders with guns did not follow us in. I rubbed my wrists and ankles to remove the droplet of blood that had formed and tried to relieve the injuries caused by the manacles and handcuffs. We were informed that we would now go through the admission procedure here at reception. The words reception and admission to me then seemed rather incongruous. Hotels have receptions and wedding parties were sometimes referred to as 'receptions'. The last institution I was 'admitted to' was the University of Cape Town.   I was also on many occasions admitted to cinemas, play houses, concerts and to be admitted you, the candidate, was a supplicant and you had to pay for admission.   This type of admission was really different.   The word 'reception' at that stage still had a rather pleasant and welcoming ring to it.   The other reception, besides the present, that might be unpleasant may be the reception to a hospital but then if you were sick that admission would be linked to hope of recovery and in that sense would still be positive. This admission had an ominous element and the personnel involved in the admission process were hostile and angry. My reverie came to an abrupt end when a warder came out and at the top of his voice shouted at us to get undressed ("trek uit!). There was then again that unexplained urgency to this process as if there was a train waiting at the other end of the corridor. Not seeing the urgency we hesitated particularly since the passage way offered no privacy and was not a place to change clothes.

The final realization that this reception was something completely different was brought home when we were aggressively and with further noise and prods from pick axe handles again told to strip off all our clothing and to face the wall. A light yellow brown shirt, pair of faded short pants and a tattered white canvass jacket were thrown at us to put on. No shoes, socks or underwear were available. Our clothes, the last vestiges of personal identity, they said, would be sent home or burnt. The State would supply clothes if we were ever released. This was put as if not very likely. The loss of identity and in particular our self actional identity was further driven home when a work group of prisoners marching in pairs came past and we were ordered by warders brandishing pick axe handles to once more turn around and face the wall We stood there on the highly polished cement floor like poverty stricken naughty children in our ill-fitting prison clothing until they passed. In the reception office we were then finger printed. My name was inscribed in a huge book and a red Prison Identity card with my name, length of sentence, prison number written on it was thrown at me. I was told to pick it up and that that the red card was my identity and to identify "maximum security prisoners" who presumably included mean and dangerous criminals like murderers and us from 'other prisoners' and not because we were regarded as communists. I certainly did not feel mean and dangerous. I then had to put my thumbprint on the card as well to personalize the card and was told to look after and protect the card. I later learnt what looking after this card meant. You, as prisoner, must ensure that you 'behave' and adhere strictly to prison regulations. Any failure or infringement of prison regulations would lead to the card being taken away which meant that you would be put on charge and if found guilty would be sentenced to deprivation of food called meal stops or, for more serious offences, to a 'carry on' (which is contrary to regulations but nevertheless applied with impunity) or to a term of solitary confinement without food or with rice water. A prisoner without a card was at risk and what this risk was I was not told and I did not feel like asking for details. It did strike me that if you did not have a card then it could not be taken away and you would be safe from solitary confinement or 'carry ons".

There was a table printed on the back of the card with 'Offence', 'punishment' and 'date' as column headings. A large purple "D" was stamped on the card signifying that I was in the very bottom prison rankings with very little privileges. I now became a number -- prisoner 88364.   Prisoner 88364 was actually the last intake of 1964 that meant that there were eight hundred and eighty-three prisoners 'admitted' to Robben Island Prison in 1964. The privileges of a D group prisoner I was told was one visit from one family member every six months and D-Group prisoners could write two approved letters per year but not exceeding five hundred words. Letters more than five hundred words would be destroyed without notification or warning. Letters should deal only with personal and family matters otherwise they would be destroyed. Letters and visits from non-family will be barred. The third and last privilege a D group could enjoy was one mug of coffee per day but if that D-group prisoner was also 'coloured' then he can have an additional mug of coffee.   During Christmas there would be an additional privilege in the form of a gift from the Prison Department but the gift would only be for that one special day. This gift, inscribed in the prison regulations, was a mug of coffee with the complements of the South African Government. I later learnt that the gift for white prisoners, in terms of the racial policy, would be a fruitcake weighing about 500 gram at Christmas. During Christmas I was also told that I could have the very special privilege of buying, from my own funds, one packet of biscuits and one packet of dried fruit but I arrived too late. I should have come in November.   All these wonderful privileges would, however, depend on good behaviour. The warder seemed to take great pleasure in announcing that I should have placed my Christmas order the previous week. But that week we were still been amused by the antics of the actors in the Supreme Court in Cape Town and the purchase of a packet of biscuits for Christmas was then far from my mind.

The government, we were told, was doing its best to help 'coloured' people get their own parliament and so would 'Indians/ Asiatic' but the Bantu (blacks) who spoke Xhosa would be getting their own country there in Transkei where they would be free as a 'nation' with their very own parliament. Blacks who spoke Sotho would get their own country as well but all Bantu (i.e. Blacks) would, however never be allowed to be citizens in South Africa.

I looked around the reception office and was amused to see an ornament of the three wise monkeys on a shelf of the "speak no evil, hear no evil, see no evil" variety. Attached to these wise monkeys was instead a little hand written note that read 'will marseer, wil studier, wil regeer' (want to march that is to fight, want to study, want to govern) which I presumed pertained to the aspirations of 'political' prisoners. We were in fact not classified as 'political prisoners' but rather as 'security' prisoners or sometimes as 'maximum security prisoners' and at other times simply as terries (i.e. terrorist) or 'bandiete' (bandits but in Afrikaans the word is sometimes used for convicts). The criminal prisoners were called 'common law prisoners' who were also called 'bandiete' or 'kriminele' to distinguish them from us. The only state acknowledged political prisoner in South Africa was Robert Sobukwe; leader of the Pan Africanist Congress (PAC) who was detained, after his three year sentence expired, by a special act of parliament. This was then renewed every year for six years until he fell ill and had to be admitted to hospital.

The warders were dressed in brown shirt and trousers with a brass emblem of the letters GDPS (standing for "Gevangenis Diens Prison Service") clipped to each shoulder. My brown shirt was more yellow and the short pants I now had on were once a yellow brown but were now very near to dirty white and badly frayed from all the washings they had been given. I took some time to examine the brass badge the warders had attached to their caps. It had a book, some type of scale and two large keys perhaps to signify 'justice' and the tools of justice (the book, the scale and keys). I thought it just needed a baton, a cat o nine tails, a flogging frame and a gallows to complete the symbolism of the then South African tools of justice. The unofficial Prison Department tools I was to discover later were pick axe handles and rubber hoses.

Opposite the reception was the office of the Head of the Prison, a warrant officer or chief warder.   The warders called him the "Opper" (meaning chief) and he called the warders 'members' meaning 'members of the Prison Service'. The incumbent at that time was Danie Theron.   A Lieutenant Colonel was the commanding officer of the Island and his office was somewhere in the 'Town' some distance away from the prison and he had majors, captains and lieutenants and warrant officers on his staff just like an army. I later came to know Danie Theron as a type of martinet who had a sneering attitude towards prisoners and who behaved as if he was Napoleon Bonaparte.   The nickname of Danie Theron amongst his warders (I mean members) was "Die Pou" (Afrikaans for the Peacock) which was very descriptive of the type of person he aspired to be.

We were then marched bare footed off to the single cells for what I later understood was an observation period although I could never imagine just what was being observed.   Attached to the door leading to the quadrangle of the single cells section was another huge brass knocker and one of the warders who escorted us banged the knocker and gave the 'dankie hek' (thank you the gate) password which reminded me of the "open sesame" incantation of the story book character Ali Baba at the mouth of the robbers' cave.   The gate was opened with a clang and we were marched into the single cell section and down the passage to the cells. I heard the gate clang shut and I wondered whether the gate would open if I should march up and called out the "dankie hek" password.   My thoughts were disturbed by a heavy shove from the back that landed me against the opposite wall of an opened cell meant for my accommodation.   First the steel gate and then the wooden door slammed shut on me.

I found myself in a small cell about two meters wide by two meters long with a barred window next to the door.   In that early evening light I could just about see a blue stone gravel courtyard through the window of the cell opposite 'my' door. The cell was thus a bit bigger than the Security Police cells in Caledon Square.

Opposite the door was another window about 50cm high by 1.5m wide about 50cm from the ceiling. In the corner was a badly battered aluminium dish with cold soft maize meal porridge that I presumed was my supper but I was not hungry enough to eat that mess. I looked up and saw a warder staring at me through the barred window next to the grill.

"Jy kan maar die kos verwyt. Wanner jy honger word sal jy dit moet vreet" (You can reject the food. When you get hungry then you will eat; except that the Afrikaans word "vreet" is the verb used to refer to eating by an animal). A mess like this was indeed to become my breakfast for the next thirteen years.

It was now early evening and a bulb encased in heavy wired glass shade fitted in the centre of the concrete ceiling dimly lighted the cell. I spent some time examining the bars on the window, the gate hinges and the huge black Union lock. The lock had screws that could be unscrewed but the slots of the screws were spot welded onto the lock casing. I tapped the bars to ensure myself that it was in fact a hollow tube. I next examined the gate more carefully. The hinge fulcrum on the gate or grill as it is called could be removed by hitting out the steel pegs of the hinges but the gate could not be moved unless unlocked and opened. I stood at the door and called to Achmad Cassiem and had an immediate response from a warder who rudely told me to "hou jou bek anders kom vat ek jou kaartjie" (shut your beak (mouth) or else I will come and take your card but he used the Afrikaans word "bek" for mouth reserved for animals). I wondered just what he would then do with my card. Achmad nevertheless responded to my greeting. A warder then appeared to tell me that there must be no talking at all. Any talking would lead to us be placed on a charge of making a noise and put on "meal stops" as punishment. ("Julle gaan maaltye kry" meaning "Your will get meals (meaning meal stops")

The dirty rope mat and three smelly blankets I found in the cell were, I supposed, meant for bedding. There was also a bottle of water and a small bucket with a lid, smelling of carbolic acid that I suppose was the toilet. I spent that first evening amusing my self by converting twelve years, to months, to days and then to hours and finally to minutes. The number appeared so big that I could not get myself to convert the number into seconds but I felt better knowing that the seconds were running down. I finally unfolded the blankets and unrolled the mat and stretched myself out on my new Grand Island styled bedding. I had to get used to the smell of the bedding and the uneven rope knots first. My mood continued to swing from one extreme to the other and at last I managed to fall asleep. A bell rang and a warder came along and woke me to tell me that the bell was the signal to sleep and anybody not sleeping would be put on charge for not sleeping. Was my sleep pattern then also to be controlled and regimented? I was now a member of the 'unfree'. I slept fitfully that first night in jail.

The following morning the clatter of a piece of iron against the bars woke me from my dreams of a free South Africa. It took me some time to realize where I was but the dark blue marks the leg irons had left on my ankles and the frayed skin on my wrists reminded me rather vividly where I was. It seemed I had slept through the wake up bell. The door to the cell was thrown open but the steel gate remained closed. I was told that next time I slept through the wake up bell I would suffer "meal stops" for forty-eight hours. I was told to roll up the sleeping mat and fold up the blankets before inspection. I was still wondering what needed to be inspected so early in the morning when some body down the passage shouted fall in and "Staan reg!" (i.e. stand right) and a warder with a more fancy cap came swaggering passed followed by other warders all of whom carried short sticks encased in leather under their arms signifying that they were officers. They asked one another if I was a new one (Is dit die nuwe een"). The "dit" corresponded to the neuter "it" which implied that as prisoners we were just a thing to them. One of the warders with a badge in the crook of the right arm turned to me and said "Waarom staan jy nie reg nie. Jy is nou 'n bandiet en jy moet dit in jou kop kry!" (Why are you not ready? You are now a bandit (prisoner) and I must get this into my head). I thought this rather funny because I thought a bandit was some type of thief. I later heard that the party that walked past was the commanding officer of the Island and his entourage doing a morning round of inspection and the term bandit or bandiet was used as a synonym for prisoner. I asked what "staan reg '(stand right) meant and what a wrong stand can be and was told that a "kriminaal" (criminal) would come and show me how to 'staan reg' which briefly made me think that "staan reg" must be something to do with crime or criminality.

A common law prisoner (the "kriminaal") was brought to show me how to fold the blankets for storage during the day. Two blankets, I am told, must first be folded into halves (i.e. folded once) and then folded once more along the same axis, the other folded thrice along the other axis. One of the twice-folded blankets must be folded once more. These must then be spread out on the floor to form a T with the thrice-folded blanket placed the crosspiece at the top. The short part of the T was then folded over to make a capital T. The fan folded blanket was then placed on the top part of the T. The two arms of the T were folded closed and the long segment of the T folded over to make a box shaped bundle. The mat was rolled into a tube and the bundle of blankets placed on top. This, I was told, was how the bedding should be folded or my card would be taken and I would be charged with untidiness. This was then the way I made my 'bed' every morning for the next thirteen years. After folding the blankets I had to dust and shine up the already shining concrete floor of the cell. The bundle of blankets shown in the picture was issued in the mid seventies as can be seen by the quality as well as the number of blankets. In the sixties there were only three flimsy blankets and a single sisal rope mat.

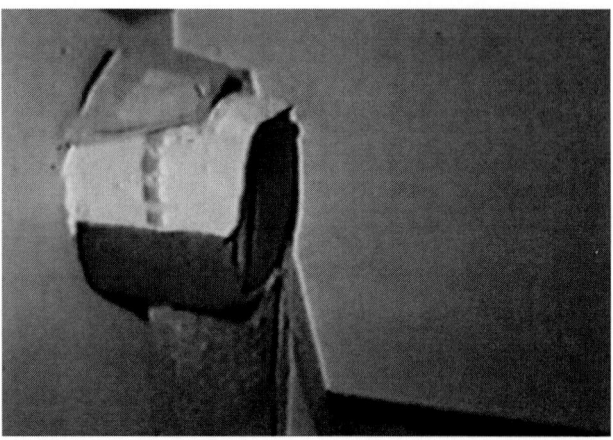

Figure 1 A luxurious set of prison bedding post 1975

In the 1960's the bedding shown in figure 1 was issued only to common law prisoners on Robben Island

A prisoner came along with dishes of maize meal porridge called "slap pap" (sloppy or soft porridge). He adroitly swung the plate of soft porridge through ninety degrees inserted it through the bars and before the porridge could fall out swung the dish back to a horizontal position inside the gate with the word "vat!" (take). I took the dish and sat down on the bundle of blankets to try and eat the fare. I noticed a few pink streaks in the off white porridge. Again I was not hungry. There was no spoon in any case. A mug of coffee was brought along later. I was not much interested in the food and after a few sips from the coffee I shoved the mug aside. I looked out of the window onto the yard and saw Mr. Mandela and company and Dr. Neville Alexander in cells on the opposite side of the courtyard. They waved and showed me the thumbs up sign. Shortly afterwards I heard a sound that appeared to be the thud of hammers on stone. Neville and his companions had started their day's work that consisted of breaking stones.

I did not work during the first two weeks except to get a supply of stones for Neville and others to break as their work.

After about ten days I was told that I was being transferred to the "seksies" (the sections), that is the communal cells. Very early the following morning I left the single cell and went to the part of the prison they called 'the Sections' (Seksies in Afrkaans). The sections were labelled Λ to D and the Afrikaans label B-Seksie amused me a little. I heard that C-section was the allocated 'study section' and I told the 'yard warder' that I wanted to study as encouraged by the Prison Department. He looked at me rather queerly as if to say that the Department did no such thing. I was nevertheless allocated to C1, the "study cell".

The warders called themselves members of the Correctional Services or members for short. Even after thirteen years I never discovered what correction they did there. The atmosphere in that prison was too negative. I imagined I could sense a form of subdued anger and frustration from the warders. The Prison was otherwise remarkably quiet except for the shouts and threats from the warders.

Like in the single cells, breakfast consisted of coffee, soft mielie (maize) meal porridge, except that I now noticed a dollop of khaki brown paste (which I was told was actually the ration of morning soup) plunked right on top of the spoon of sugar that went with the porridge. I got a wooden spoon from one of the comrades by the name of Zambotla. No metal spoons were allowed for 'security reasons' and prisoners made these wooden spoons themselves. My first spoon was a short handled type looking more like a small ladle. The spoon was kept in the top pocket of the prison jacket and carried around like an emergency tool. The spoon was only washed during the evening when access to a tap in the cell was possible. I decided to try and eat to preserve my strength and nutritional status. I forced the food down suppressing a gag that welled up from the pit of my stomach.

After breakfast I was, with a party of other new comers, told to go to the store in the Zinc section to get my supplies. It seemed that the clothing I had on belonged to the single cell section and needed to be returned. During that time no D-group prisoner walked anywhere even in the courtyard without being escorted by a warder. If the prisoner left the confines of the fence that surrounded the prison, then the escort must also be properly armed – a revolver if there were less than four prisoners, a Belgian automatic rifle with forty bullets if there were more than three prisoners to 'protect'. I thought that this perhaps this had something to do with the number of bullets available from each of these types of firearms.

I was escorted to the store by a young warder. I had to walk in front so that he could keep an eye on me from the back. The warder must have noticed the way I looked at the fence because he then told me that if I cross that fence then I would be dead since that was the deadline and I remembered how many times during my student years the due dates of assignments and tutorials were called 'deadlines'. Here the deadlines were literal. At the store I first had to present my prison identity card with the large D stamped on it signifying my qualification to receive an issue of clothing of the lowest caste. Common law prisoners enter prison as C groups and they were demoted only if they caused trouble. Maximum security prisoners like us were classified as D groups on entry to the prison with promotion at the discretion of the Prison Board which was based on' behaviour' as was clearly stated to me by the warder at the reception.

Remission of sentence was also at the discretion of the Prison Board as stated on my identity card by the word "Raad" next to the words "With remission". Even the date of discharge had the word "Raad" next to it implying the Prison Board would decide on the date of release irrespective of sentence. There was in fact no thought of remission and, as far as I know, no 'security' prisoner ever got remission. I stayed the full term of twelve years plus the additional sentence added for 'bad' behaviour and even this addition had no remission. At the store I was issued with three flimsy blankets and a rope mat encased in a liberal amount of grime for bedding. A towel the size and material of a dishcloth was provided for drying after a shower. I was further given a black felt hat, navy blue socks with two bright red stripes at the top and an odd pair of shoes – one size nine and the other a size six. The sole of the shoes was made from an old motorcar tyre and I thought that my footsteps would be now like tyre tread marks. Feeling a bit like Oliver Twist I protested that I normally wear size seven shoes. This request elicited a loud yell from the warder of the store:

"Bandiet! Ek besit jou gat en jy 's nou innie blerrie tronk en hier het jy geen regte hoor jy, geen blerrie regte en jy kan die duiwel dank vir die blerrie skoene" (Prisoner, I own your arse and you are now in the bloody jail and here you have no bloody rights do you hear, no bloody rights and you can thank the Devil for the bloody shoes).

The common law prisoner who seemed to be the assistant store man emphasized that I was lucky to get a pair of shoes and I must 'vat en loop' (take and go). Further, I was seriously reminded by a common law prisoner who I surmised was actually more of the 'deputy' store man not to address the Baas (master) (meaning the warder) as mister but as baas (boss or master).

Most of my comrades had sandals. In tune with the racial policy of the South African Nationalist Party Government black prisoners were given sandals and not shoes or socks and in place of a black hat they were issued with a cloth cap. When I later learnt the hat or cap was issued purely so that you could take it off when you spoke to a warder or when 'on parade' I exchanged the hat for a cap. A cap could be folded and put in the pocket. I was not going to be bothered by the "hats off, hats on" games. I was further given an off white canvass jacket, a well-worn pairs of flannel short pants that were once khaki and now almost dirty cream, and a khaki shirt. No underwear was issued to 'D-diet' (coloured) and 'F-diet' (Black) prisoners. For toiletries I was given a piece of blue soap and a piece of red carbolic soap and a razorless blade for shaving. The red soap was for bathing and the blue soap for washing clothes. My identity card, which I had to submit to the store man in order to get all these goodies, was now thrown on the floor at my feet for me to pick up. It seemed that I was now not human enough for the card to be handed to me. It was below the dignity of the store warder to put my identity card into my hand.

I now had to submit to a hair cut. The Common law prisoner who was the 'assistant' store man wanted to cut my hair to the scalp with a hair clipper. I stopped him when he wanted to shave my head with a blade and he went to tell his 'baas'. When his boss came I told him that the prison regulation said that hair must be neat and it does not refer to shaving the head. He told me that I must not try to be clever (slim trek) otherwise I would see my arse (jy sal gou jou gat sien) and I better 'fok' off from his store. With the baldhead I became a true bandiet.   All the time this was taking place my warder escort said nothing and just stood opposite the door. All of us who were at the store picked up our goodies to take to the cells where we were to stay and the escort just trailed behind.

By the time all this was finished all the labour gangs were gone and I was told by the Yard warder that my work for that day would be to help clean and polish the passage way to the cells in B Section.   The naming of the sections was subsequently changed. The yard warder then announced to no one in particular "Daai amper baas (presumably meaning me) gaan môre gwarrie toe" (That almost boss will go to the quarry tomorrow). I believed that I was called an "amper baas" because as a "coloured" I was thought of as a mixture of White and Black ancestors and therefore half a baas. I was told a common law prisoner would show me how to do the cleaning. I was then escorted to B section. That was the part of the prison that required the contribution of my effort to clean. When I arrived at my first place of labour I found the assigned common law prisoner putting dabs of polish on the bare concrete floor that was already shining from an infinite number of previous cleaning efforts and the latest effort could very well have been the day before. The warder who escorted me then wondered off.

A cellblock or Section consisted of four cells forming an H with the access passage forming the cross piece of the H linking the cells. This cross piece also provided the entrance to the section. We had to concentrate on cleaning this cross piece that day. Other cleaners were busy cleaning the cells. My 'foreman' appeared to be a rather morose person with tear drops tattooed just below his eyes displaying a type of mental cowering when warders were present. He also had ever shifting eyes. I wondered later, after learning more about prison psychology, if these were symptoms of the paranoia characteristic of the prisoner suffering from 'prison psychosis' caused by long term imprisonment as referred to in psychology textbooks. Peter Stokes (for that was the name of my 'foreman' that day) also had a tattoo of a hammer and sickle on his forearm that he called a 'tchupp' (the Cape Flats Afrikaans for a rubber stamp derived from the sound a rubber stamp makes when it hits paper). He seemed very proud of this tchupp.

Tattoos or tchupps seemed to be mandatory with common law prisoners. I saw others with tears permanently tattooed on their face. I think this may represent Peter Stokes' response to his imprisonment since he always greeted everybody with the words "Hard times Pellie" using the Afrikaans diminutive for pal and used as a term of endearment. In the communal bathroom I once saw a common law prisoner with a mouse tattooed on his buttock scurrying to the one and only opening available between the twin mounds of flesh. I later learnt that tattoos were the hallmark of the long term prisoner and I wondered if I would also end up with a tchupp.

I joined my 'foreman' in dabbing polish on to the floor until the floor looked like a large malnourished leopard skin. When this was done we spread the polish using brooms. After this my 'mentor' threw two pieces of old blankets at me. He told me to put these on the floor and stand on it. He did the same and then proceeded to slide on the cloth in a rhythmic fashion like someone trying to skate but without lifting the feet. I followed his lead. A minute later he began to chant to give us both a work rhythm. For the next three hours we glided crosswise to and fro, up and down the passage to the monotonous chant repeated ad nauseum 'die plek se naam is tronk, ... die plek se naam is tronk, ...' (the name of the place is jail, ... the name of the place is jail). The state and security police could not have designed a better brain washing session. This place was indeed a jail, I was trapped in it and this was now been drummed into my consciousness and further down into my sub conscious. I became mesmerized by this chant. I woke with a start and decided there and then that this was not going to sink further into my spirit.

I had to refocus my mind and whilst sliding up and down the floor I began to study the environment seeking in it for a source of distraction.

I noted the guards armed with Belgian automatic rifles on the posts and on a catwalk in front of the single cells section. The prison itself consisted of four of the H-shaped stone buildings with asbestos roofs called sections and labeled A to D. The yard was strewn with coarse white lime mixed with chipped seashells. The kitchen was on one side of the Sections and the single cell accommodation and Hospital (still then in the process of been built) on the other side towards the front. One of the two chimneys on top of the kitchen was belching black smoke. Between the Hospital and the single cells, but a little further to the front, was the reception office and armoury. A double-layered two metre high barbed wire fence surrounded the prison and a diamond mesh fence separated the kitchen from the sections. There were two gates in this fence - one for entering and another for exiting the kitchen area. At each corner of the prison and in the centre of the yard were tall blue stone watch towers with armed guards standing at the windows on top. Halfway between the ground and the window of each watch tower was a square hole to poke a gun or small cannon through. On the right hand side of the prison was a fence separating the stone prison (Klip tronk) from the Zinc section (called the Blik tronk – Afrikaans for tin jail) where most of the common law prisoners were held. In the earlier days the hospital was also accommodated in the Zinc Section. The Zinc Section was constructed out of corrugated roofing sheets and consisted of a set of cells surrounding an enclosed courtyard. The Zinc Section was later demolished to give way to a sports and recreation area that included the Rugby field/ soccer field.

Ironically, when I gazed around round the prison, I again experienced a queer sense of relief to be out of the hands of the security police and their one by two metre prison cells, their chalk circles, their rubber batons, their electric shock generators and their endless questions and threats. One of their threats was Robben Island where there would be much suffering. This threat for me had now become a reality. It was great to see the 'goodly sun' and feel the wider open spaces despite the oppressive restriction of prison with its atmosphere of latent violence.

We were later joined by "Uil" (the Afrikaans for Owl) another common law prisoner whose job was to clean the cell towards the front. Uil came to look for a lighter (or "hond" as he called it) to light his brown paper hand rolled cigarette and also to chat a bit. In the early days only common law prisoners were "qualified" to become cleaners. Uil was also a gang member. Like Uil I also then had a gap in my front teeth and this attracted his attention. He wanted to know if I want the gap filled because he is going to have his gap filled with gold to spell out his name (Uil) so that if he "smiles people then will know who they smiling with". After talking about where the supply of tobacco would come from tonight at 7:00 and who to 'check out' Uil left to go back to his place of work. Check out I gathered meant who to speak to for a supply of tobacco. Seven o'clock was the time the 'monitors' came in and they are the upper class of prison society. Each monitor had a large brass M or a star like a sheriff on his chest that gave him freedom of movement in and around town and the prison. They had the best jobs and had access to tobacco and other goodies. These monitors did not actually monitor anything.

After some time I noticed my 'mentor' looking at me rather curiously. It seemed that this attention was sparked off Uil's reference to the gap in my teeth. This gap was then a characteristic of the people of the Cape. The water was said to have been too pure to supply the necessary minerals to develop healthy teeth amongst the poor and the working class tended to loose teeth very early and the gap may very well be my badge of membership to this class. I had a partial dental plate but this was damaged by the police.

"Have you joined a (prison) gang yet", he asked me rather abruptly. I said no and asked him what my options were and I then had my first lesson in prison lore. He told me that there were at least eight gangs on Robben Island to choose from. He then proceeded to enumerated these as the Twenty-six, the Twenty-eight, the Desperadoes, the Big Five, the Big Six, the African National Congress (ANC), and the Poqos (Pan Africanist Congress or PAC) and each of these gangs he told me had their code that he called their "Book" that I later learnt referred to their policy and rules. There was no real book. You could recognize each gang, he said, by how they saluted one another. I was intrigued to hear the ANC and the PAC (the Poqo) listed by him as 'gangs'. The Twenty-six, he told me, saluted one another by lifting the small finger of the right hand and calling out "Sickies!" (probably derived from the six of twenty-six) and he lifted his hand with his thumb and fingers, except the little one, curled into a fist to demonstrate, giving the little finger a jaunty shake. The little finger was regarded as the sixth finger and that was the theory behind that type of salute. The ANC, he said, saluted one another by lifting the fist in almost the same manner as the Desperadoes except that the ANC called out "Amandla!" to be answered with "Awethu" and the Desperadoes called out "Des!" to be answered by a "des". For the Desperadoes the fist, he said, meant "moer end donder" (punch and beat up) but he admitted not knowing what the fist meant for the ANC, perhaps it was the same, he said.   Sometimes the ANC lifted the thumb with the words "Maije boeije" (this was actually a different section of the ANC). The PAC saluted by presenting the palm and calling out, as he put it "Zwelethu"; to be answered by "iAfrika" and the Big Six saluted by stamping their feet and swinging their right hand to the side of their forehead sometimes calling out "Alles reg!" (Alls right). Here his knowledge of the theory of salutes broke down completely. This intrigued me even more. It seemed that the warders were in fact the Big Six Gang. My "mentor" thus saw the warders as just another prison gang. This was affirmed when he explained the relations between the Big Six and the Big Five and the other gangs.

The 'book' of the Big Five said that they must assist the Big Six by keeping them informed of everything that happened in the Prison.   They acted as the informers or, as he called them, "pimps".   To pimp meant to inform authorities of what was happening in the prison and had nothing to do with prostitutes. Pimping was the "book" or "policy" of the Big Five. He then warned me to be on my guard with the Big Fives and he waved the small and index fingers of his right hand with the two middle fingers and thumb folded down in front of his eyes to make the action of looking out with both the eyes more graphic.

Gangs also had their own emblems. The Big Five's emblem was the swastika. Like Hitler, they could not be trusted. He told me that he himself was a Desperado and their emblem was the hammer and the sickle and he proudly showed me a tattoo of a hammer and sickle on his right shoulder. I asked him if they were Russians and Communists and he said yes one could call them Russian but he did not know anything about communists having never even heard the word.

There was also another gang called the "Air Force" but they were not represented on Robben Island. The 'Book' of the Air force said that they must always try to escape (that is to fly, hence the name 'Air force). On Robben Island there could be no escape and there was therefore no "Air Force" there. He said that he was once a member of the Air force when he was in a prison on the mainland. He then further explained that you could not escape from here because of the sharks in the sea and the water was too cold. I already knew that the bars were cut proof. Each bar consisted of a steel tube with an inner solid steel bar mounted on ball bearings set deep within the concrete windowsill and frame. If you cut through the outer tube the inner bar would just roll with the saw.

I now set myself the task of pondering a method to cut these "ultra maximum security bars" and it struck me that the bars could indeed be cut if the tools were available. I would cut the tube in two places and then use a screw jack to jam the now loose outer tube tightly onto the inner bar thus using the outer tube as a brake to keep the inner bar firm and steady for cutting. I wondered if I would ever have the opportunity to try this.

I then asked my 'mentor' where and how did one sign on to join his gang for example. He again gave me a rather queer look and told me if I wanted to join the Desperadoes then the Leader or "General" would give me a task as an initiation to prove my worth. Such a task could be, for example, finding and smashing the face and head of a rival gang member with a spade or making a makeshift knife and stabbing someone preferably a Big Five member with it. If I was lucky the general might give me an easier task such as to grab the Prison Commander's cap when he came along for Sunday inspection and to trample on it. I tried to picture this and to imagine what would then happen. Would he just brush of his cap when I explained the reason? If the task was successfully carried out then the "judges" of the gang would recommend to the leader whether the neophyte could be accepted as a fully fledged member with all the rights and privileges such as protection and the allocation of a space in the communal cells and to trade for tobacco.

I was intrigued to learn that the gangs also had judges and I could not resist asking him what other functions the judges served and he explained that the judges also heard cases brought against a member if the member committed an offence against the gang's rules or 'book' and would then decide on the member's guilt or otherwise. The judges might also judge and condemn members of rival gangs, even in absentia. I then wanted to know what punishments might for example be metered out to the guilty and he told me that for lighter offences the guilty might be sentenced to say ten smacks in the face or to 50 mugs of water. In the latter instance the accused as punishment must drink fifty mugs of water in one sitting. He told me that he once saw this water punishment being administered in the cell and after that the convicted walked around like a drunk. I remembered having read somewhere that excess water in the system could, as was the case with water torture, lead to some form of intoxication. The water torture was used by the Japanese during the Second World War and consisted of connecting the victim's mouth to a high-pressure hose. The death sentence, my 'mentor' pointed out, was reserved for serious offences but I could not get a clear indication what 'serious offences' were. Even members of other gangs could be sentenced to death. Death sentences against other gang members seemed some form of reprisal against the foreign gang when there was a war against that gang. I now asked my mentor about the other duties of the "judges" and who the prosecutors and defence were but the bell rang for lunch and my first lesson in prison lore came to an end. I later met the Head or the 'general' of the Desperadoes during one of my terms in the punishment cells and I was able to have extensive discussions with him.

Lunch was at one o'clock and this consisted of maize grit called mealie rice or in Afrikaans "mielie gruis" with a boiled onion on top and a handful of partly cooked beans. It could be seen why this maize grit was called mielie rys and then translated into English as mealie rice and back into Afrikaans as "mealie rys". This mealie 'rice' we collected at the kitchen. The F-diets were given a plate of coarse maize (still in their cellulose jackets) mixed with a small amount of beans. A drink called 'puza mandla' was also served to F-diet prisoners. After collecting our food at the kitchen we were conducted to a cell in the Zinc section to go and enjoy our fare. I settled down and tried to eat this food. I took a wooden spoon full of my 'rice' with beans. Chewing my first spoonful was interrupted by sudden sharp pain. I bit on a stone in the beans and I felt as if I had broken a tooth. The stones were well 'camouflaged' to look like beans. They were the same dark khaki brown colour as the beans. I learnt that each subsequent spoon must be very carefully checked. This was done, I was told, by listening carefully whilst sliding the next spoon of the food back and forth on the metal dish. A grating sound would signify that there was another stone present. This stone needed to be located and removed before eating further. The stones probably got into the beans when they were harvested and since the beans were meant for prisoners, no effort was made to clean the beans. Sometimes cow peas replaced the beans. Cow peas were slightly bigger that ordinary peas but brown in colour and very chewy. They take a long time to cook. The advantage of cow peas was that they contained less stones and the stones in cow peas were less cunningly camouflaged. During lunch some of my foreman's friends came to sit with us and I listened with some amusement at the story my mentor, in very colourful Afrikaan, was telling them about how he met his girl friend before he was arrested.

After lunch it was again 'die plek se naam is tronk' up and down the already shimmering concrete floor of the passage of B-Section. The cleaner of the passage of A section came to visit us.

He too came to borrow a "hond" or cigarette lighter from my 'foreman'. This was a device consisting of a piece of flint and a prison issued tooth brush used for lighting hand rolled brown paper cigarettes called 'zolls'. The handles of prison issued toothbrushes were remarkably inflammable. It seemed that it was made of an older variety of plastic/celluloid, which I remembered could even be explosive. The irony of these explosive substances in an apartheid prison intrigued me. Shavings of the tooth brush handle were obtained by rubbing it against a piece of rough cement. The flint was struck against a rough surface until a spark landed into the cellulose shavings causing them to catch alight and glow bright enough to light a zoll. Smoking was strictly prohibited except for A and B group prisoners who could have tobacco, cigarettes and lighters in their possession. Other groups had to smuggle their tobacco or ask for 'donations' from the A or B groups. They, at risk of been caught, sometimes kept their own "dogs" for lighting their 'zolls'. I was immensely grateful not to have been a smoker. Smokers, especially if they were acutely addicted, had a particularly difficult time in prison and prison warders and their officers (that is the Big Six) were prepared to exploit this weakness to its fullest. This was one of our biggest vulnerabilities as a community.

The afternoon lesson from my 'mentor' was an exposition about work in the quarry and how tough it was there and what other prison work options there were. Work was classified as "light labour", "suitable labour" or "hard labour" depending on your medical report. To be a light or suitable labourer you needed a certificate from the prison doctor. There was an agricultural work span (called 'Landbou" – the Afrikaans for Agriculture) but they did not plant anything since there was no water for irrigation. I thought my foreman was joking, but he assured me that that was what they in fact did. The Big Six disliked the Poqos and there was a continuous war between them. Then there was the Washing Span but I did not stand a chance of getting in there since it was for older or sickly prisoners only and washing thus was classified as "suitable Labour". The Shoemaker Span needed a skill that I did not have. The same problem existed with the Building Span (Bou-groep). I did not even know what a brick looked like. The cleaners (who polish up the cell floors and passage floors) were regarded as "light labourers" and reserved for common law prisoners. There are prisoners who worked in the town, the shop, the officer's mess, the single quarters and the streets of Robben Island Town that needed cleaning. All work in town was very strictly reserved for common law prisoners only. The reason for this was that 'Poqos' (i.e. Security Prisoners) stole newspapers and newspapers were the ultimate contraband. Newspaper smuggling was thus a 'hanging offence' and was at the same level as cocaine smuggling or even worse. Before my transportation to Robben Island I would never have been able to imagine the sensation of walking across the Prison yard with a news paper cutting in my pocket. It felt as if it could easily burn a hole through my trousers. Occasionally common law prisoners who worked in town stole goods or money from the shop or from the residences but this was by far not as serious as smuggling newspapers. There was a case of a common law prisoner committing adultery with a warder's wife but even this was not as serious as smuggling newspapers. I was in any case destined for hard labour in the quarry since the Big Six did not seem to like me. In the quarry I would 'sweat my guts out in summer and freeze my butt off in winter' and would come back in the evening too tired even to piss. Nevertheless I was told that "Daar gaan jy kak!" (There you will shit) meaning that there I would truly suffer.

At about four o'clock a bell rung and we were instructed to 'fall in'. We lined up in front of the kitchen gate and waited for the rest of the prisoners to arrive from their respective work places. A morose, very dusty and tired looking quarry gang came in through the big gates. I could see the fatigue in their faces and amusement in the face of the criminals who had special privileges even in the quarry. We were now joined by various spans from other areas of work. At the command 'stap uit!' we moved into the kitchen terrain with the shouts "D-Diet one side". As a D-diet I was given a quarter loaf of bread called a 'cutkop' with a thin layer of hard fat on one side, a mug of soup and a mug of coffee that appeared to have been made from a mixture of burnt teak and ordinary saw dust. The 'F-diets were served with the same type of porridge they had for breakfast except there was a boiled onion riding on top of the metal dish of porridge. I once asked why the difference and was told that the prison department policy was to provide the standard to which each 'race' was used to. It was explained that blacks for example do not wear shoes or eat bread outside hence providing bread would result in a black prisoner living at a higher standard than an average black outside prison and so it was for all the elements and resources of living.

I still remember that porridge with the distinctly musty taste and the occasional pinkish streaks - the carcasses of worms or maggots that once lived in the maize meal before it was cooked to death and served up as porridge. At I first felt nauseous but by the end of my first month in prison I was used to this and the diarrhoea that I believed was caused by the pink streaks, stopped. I developed my resistance.

After eating supper kneeling with one leg on the ground in the gravel covered square next to the kitchen we were marched off in two's to our cells. I went to C1 that was the study cell. Inside the cell we once more made two parallel lines. The yard warder came with his book to count us and noted the number down in this book and I thought of miser Scrooge who counted his money so often. First the iron-gate (the grill) and then the steel door was firmly closed on us and locked with a distinctive clang. The warders left and a type of relief descended on us. We were now left to our own devices but for some it was more of a deep sense of gratitude that they survived yet another day. For me the real fight for survival would start the following day and I looked forward to this with some trepidation and also a sense of challenge.

In the cell I met Ephraim Bahula, Indries Naidoo, Stanley Magoba, Nick Kekane, Sambotla and Marcus Solomons and all the rest who would be my family for the next thirteen years. I also met Dimake Malepe, the son of Professor Malepe of the University of South Africa barely sixteen years old with a life sentence, Dikgang Moseneke aged sixteen and the son of a well known High School principal in Gautemg with a ten year sentence 'affixed to his name' to use the terminology of the warrants issued by the courts. There were formal introductions and hand clasping and I was asked to give a brief description of who I was and an overview of the situation 'outside'. Sambotla undertook to be my mentor to show me around and to try and protect me to make my transition to prison easier. There was no formal allocation of mentorship. We just took to one another – a kind of sub vocal understanding and liking for one another.

In the cell C1 there were about fifty prisoners, about five ANC, one YCC and the rest were PAC. Tony Suze who became my brother there on Robben Island was at that time in another cell. He still had to get permission to study before he would be allowed to come to C-Section. I still had to get permission to study but I told the warders that I was going to C1 and they did not question this.

The cell C1 was as all cells in the Sections a medium size hall capable of holding about fifty prisoners sleeping in two rows lying feet to feet with a narrow footpath between to accommodate shoes when we were finally allowed to take shoes into the cell. The floor was highly polished concrete and the ceiling was grey painted concrete and the walls neutral grey. Large bulbs supplied light in white glass shades suspended from the ceiling making the cell fairly well lit. Low wattage bulbs encased in a wired glass fitting very dimly lighted the other cells. Along one side of the cell were fifteen work surfaces for writing on about 60 cm by 50cm at a height of about one metre and slanted at twenty degrees to the horizontal, all next to one another. Each work surface was a lid covering a book storage space. The whole arrangement was mounted on steel tubes cemented into the wall. We called this our desks. Prisoners had to stand and read. I once asked why chairs were not provided and was told that if chairs were provided we may come to think of ourselves as Menere (Misters). Those who could not stand and read for too long went into the bathroom and sat on a mat rolled into a tube to serve as a makeshift 'stool' and stood up in front of a wash basin covered with a piece of hardboard serving as a desk.

Somebody clapped his hands and quiet descended over the cell. It was study period. I borrowed a book to read. An hour later the same person clapped his hands to signify that study period was over and conversation started again. This was the daily after work routine in the cells. At eight o'clock the bell rang to tell prisoners that they must now sleep. Only those who had study privileges were allowed to stay awake until ten o'clock when a warder would come and flick the lights to indicate that it was time to sleep. I once asked a warder what the charge would be if I did not sleep. His simple answer was that "Jy sal jou gat sien" (You will then see your arse). There appeared to be a visible conflict on the part of the warders. They would have loved to switch off the lights so that no one could read but as pointed out earlier in a Maximum Security Prison lights were never switched off. Those who wanted to study or read later than ten had to hide in the bathroom or set up blankets at the door where they could not be seen by the warders who came to look through the passage window to check on us. Sambotla came to speak to me quietly before sleeping time. He brought me a new wooden spoon, that he had made himself, as a gift. We talked about our previous existence, the problems we had had with the police and what our thoughts were about the future. Little did I then know that he as a person did not have a future. To-morrow it would be hard labour 'gwarrie' but Zambotla said that he would be there to help if necessary. I had finished my first two weeks in prison.

We then prepared for sleep. The thin rope mat and three worn-out and smelly blankets were spread open. Two blankets as sheets and one as a cover in summer. In winter two or even three blankets was not enough to serve as cover and we would then packed together to share heat. No cushions were issued and I folded up my shirt and short pants to serve as a makeshift cushion. No pyjamas were issued either and you had to sleep naked. Before clearing my mind for sleep I thought of the four thousand three hundred and eighty two days still left – unless I come up with a plan or the revolution speeds up. I slept sporadically on my mat and from time to time I heard the guards on the watch tower singing out "Alles reg" or "Wie gaan daar" (Alls right or who goes there) as their officers came pass for the regular inspections throughout the night. The bedding was uncomfortable and smelly which made sleeping not very easy. Sambotla told me not to worry much about the blankets. He will help me wash them during the weekend. Prison blankets, he told me, must be washed carefully otherwise the wool will came out and the blanket will become thread bare and even more inadequate than old blankets and this will be a problem during the harsh winters to come. I looked around in the gloom of the cell at the bundles of dark grey blanket covering my fellow prisoners each one in his private world of thought or sleep. Blues (Ncanda) who always tended to see humour once remarked that we looked like a herd of reclining donkeys under our grey blankets.

The lights remained on the whole night and that was another disturbance. Some of us slept with the blanket over our heads as a shield against the light. I could not breathe under the blanket so I folded the upper part of the blanket just to shield my eyes from the light but keeping my nose sticking out for air. After my release I read an article in a Medical Journal that stated that regular periods of darkness are necessary for the body to rest properly. The darkness has something to do with melanin levels. I wonder then what effect these years of lack of darkness had on us and again I worried about the after effects of the long term imprisonment will have on us and how we can resist it.

That night I again spent the time before sleeping thinking of escape and of the people I left behind. I still had no idea how escape could be achieved. I needed more information and for that I needed to get to see the Zinc Section since the Sheets of corrugated zinc that made up the walls of this section must be more vulnerable than the steel and concrete which encase us in the "Klip Tronk" (Stone Jail). During that time the Hospital was still housed in the Zinc Section and I thought that pretending to be sick may make a short stay there in the hospital possible. This did not work too well. My stay in the hospital was too short and it was very difficult to keep up the pretence of being sick. A number of Big Fives members stayed in the Zinc Jail particularly in the Hospital where they are sheltered and given special privileges by their allies and masters the Big Six and they gave detailed reports of what transpired in the hospital cell.

Chapter 4

First Day in the Yard

The bell rang at 0500 the following morning. Immediately after the bell the PAC members broke into one of their freedom songs to meet the new day; the PAC salute of Izwelethu (our Country) was called out by somebody followed by the chorus of response "iAfrika" (the prescribed reaction). A statement of re-dedication to the struggle followed, with the words: "Forward then to independence, to independence now, tomorrow the giant monolithic state of Africa" whilst members of the ANC looked on passively. We took turns in groups of about nine to go to the communal bathroom and toilet adjoining the cell. At about six o'clock a warder outside shouted "Fall in" (in English even though they speak Afrikaans exclusively, refusing or unable to speak any other English) and we made two parallel lines in the middle of the cell. First the metal door, then the iron grill were noisily opened and the Warder in charge of the Yard entered with his book and, accompanied by two warders brandishing pick axe handles, counted us. I mentally counted with him where I stood and came to an answer of sixty-four, the same number as last night. We were then told us to "stap uit" (step out). In this manner we were then counted every morning and evening. Over the years I noticed that the more hostile warders counted our feet as if they could not bear to look at our faces, the better warders counted our shoulders. At the door of the cell and down the passage way more warders stood with threatening batons drawn. Many unfortunate prisoners would get a clout over the head or shoulders for no apparent reason except that they were perhaps moving too slowly or not looking ahead since the assault was followed by the words "stap uit" (step out, meaning walk faster) or "kyk voor" (look ahead). We crossed the yard in pairs with warders shouting at us, urging us to keep in pairs even though we were walking in two's, and again "kyk voor, agter is donker" (look ahead, it is dark behind you) seemed to be the reason to keep on looking ahead, "bly stil (keep quiet) could be heard even though nobody talked and I wondered why it should be dark behind us and I made a point to myself to ask this. Looking sideways never mind behind would attract a clout from the pickaxe handle.   It felt like we were 'walking the gauntlet'. There was no talking in the yard and the still early morning air was tense and quiet, punctured by the screams of the warders interspersed with the higher pitched shout of the seagulls wheeling overhead all urging the rows of quiet shuffling prisoners to keep moving and to keep quiet as if there was a level of quiet beyond quiet.

The morning air had a promise of a magnificent early summer day in Cape Town. The school and University holidays had started and the beautiful beaches of Cape Town were inviting the indolent of the City to its sand and sun, but for us there was going to be no holiday making here was the rather odd thought than crossed my mind that morning whilst hurrying across the coarse grey gravel yard of Robben Island Prison. We had embraced the revolution and that was and would be the focus of our lives – it was in fact like a career move.

No walking in the yard was allowed unless in pairs or "Twee-twee" in Afrikaans. A warder with an ascetic looking face and a blank stare was at regular intervals calling out "twee-twee" as if it was his mating call. I later came to know this warder, whose name was Marais, but better known by his nickname "Ekwilbou" (meaning I want to build) and even then he showed psychotic tendencies. He was in charge of the "Bou Group Span" (building span or work group) and the urge to build was another of his compulsions. "Stap uit met daai kruiwa, ek wil bou!". (Step out meaning hurry with that wheel barrow, I want to build) I was told could be heard the whole day at the building site where he was in charge. I was never privileged enough to work in that Building Span and this was thus purely hear-say. I believed that Ekwilbou finally became human in 2001. Tony Suze who served a sentence of fifteen years told me that Ekwilbou later came to him in Pretoria long after his release to ask for forgiveness for his behaviour towards us when he was a warder on Robben Island. This was rather ironic since we considered him to be one of the better warders.

Another of the petty harassments was the fixation with buttons. Buttons had to be done up and a prisoner with any undone shirt or jacket button forfeited his meal or attracted a clout on the head with a pick-axe handle for this 'misdemeanour'. The kitchen area was a 'holy' zone to be entered with great deference and respect. Prisoners must wear jackets to enter the area to get food and the jacket in particular must be buttoned up as far as there are buttons. Only if the jacket lacks a button will the prisoner be exempted from this but warned that the button better be in place next time.

At the kitchen gate the two lines diverged around a large wire tray from which we hastily had to grab a metal mug (two mugs if you were a D-diet prisoner since D-diets were also entitled to a mug of coffee) before mounting the kitchen stoep where the serving hatch was. We shuffled along, still in pairs, towards the serving hatch on the stoep where a plate of cold porridge made from ground maize meal was hastily shoved in our hands followed by the words "Hak" (which is the idiomatic Afrikaans for clear off and a bit milder than fuck off) as each pair got to the head of the queue to receive their plates. The haks were heard as monotonous as clockwork occasionally broken with "Vat die blerrie pap" (take the bloody porridge) when somebody fumbled at the hatch. This went on until every prisoner was served.

The off white porridge had a brown paste on it (which I was informed was our ration of soup) with a ration of sugar floating on top of the 'soup'. We then stepped down into another queue to have our mugs filled with coffee. D-diets (which I then knew to be another name for 'coloureds') were allowed to step aside to have another spoon of sugar added to their porridge. On one side stood the warder in charge of the kitchen, like a first class chef, proudly watching us taking the fare that was concocted under his supervision. We then proceeded, in the early morning gloom under floodlights, to form neat lines in the open air square next to the kitchen. Guards armed with automatic rifles stood just outside the fence. Each prisoner ate crouching with one knee touching the ground to maintain balance with the noisy gulls still frolicking overhead under the brightening sky of rose pink and isolated white morning clouds. If you were lucky, you might have your porridge fertilized by the gulls from above possibly to augment the dubious nutrient content of the porridge whilst the warders with their pick axe handles and batons at the ready moved around and between the group of eating prisoners as if each of us might stand up and rush them; or perhaps they thought prisoners had to be forced fed since occasionally one would say "Vreet julle Poqos" (vreet is the Afrikaans verb to eat applied to animals). I think these warders with their petty minds enjoyed the sense of power derived from harassing us and this realization somehow made me feel less angry.

Additional guards armed with automatic rifles at ready stood watching us from a wooden platform about three metres high in the space across the double barbed wire fences surrounding the prison. The harassment continued without any let up. The intimidation from the warders always seemed to be accompanied by the shriek from the sea birds gliding gracefully above our dining field. I dabbed my spoon into the "soup" and recalled my 'foreman' of yesterday's advice not to eat the soup since it contained a drug that suppressed sex drive and would ultimately make prisoners sterile. The purple green streaks, he said, was evidence of the presence of the drug he said.

Whilst forcing the 'pap' down trying my best to watch out for pink streaks that could add unwanted protein to the meal, I looked around and thought our dining field looked rather poverty stricken covered with chips of blue stone, next to the kitchen where coal for the boilers was off loaded. Words such "kaffer", "coolie", hotnot (referring to Black, Indians and Coloured respectively), "kyk voor agter is donker" continued unabated as a form of breakfast entertainment for us. Suddenly I noticed a change in the sound pattern. From behind I heard the words: "Meintjies, de Jager, kom kyk hiers 'n amper baas" (Meintjies, de Jager (come and see here is a half Boss - presumably me) and a troop of warders gathered behind me. The rimless spectacles I was wearing may have contributed to the curiosity. I felt myself being inspected with great inquisitiveness and I came to know a bit of what a monkey in a zoo must feel like.

After five minutes two rows at a time in turn were told to get up and march in pairs (so as to maintain the twee-twee theme) to the square on the other side of the kitchen, where the Hall was to be built in a later year, to queue up in their allocated work group lines. If you did not swallow the food in the time allowed, you had to leave it (hungry or not). Chief warder, van Tonder, who came a few years later took great delight in grabbing the dish of porridge from still hungry prisoners so that he could feed the sea gulls earning for himself the nick name "Sopapa" from the word pap meaning soft porridge. Sopapa also went under the alternate nickname of "Cutkop". A cutkop refers to the quarter loaf of brown bread issued to D-diet prisoners for supper. Van Tonder earned himself the nickname when he started grabbing bread from D-diet prisoners who did not eat all their bread at supper in the prescribed time of five minutes to feed to his sea gulls. The irony, to me, was that according to the warders who spoke to me, the malicious Chief Warder van Tonder was very a religious Christian and also a lay priest. During my 'off' periods I sometimes thought that perhaps his Christianity was simply reserved for whites only.

Those who worked in the washing span formed their double line; the agriculture group (landbou) formed their line. Sambotla, my guide and mentor, came to show me to the quarry span standing next to the barbed wire fence. The quarry span was the largest of the work groups and they stood in fours thus breaking the 'Twee-twee' theme unless this was considered a double twee-twee.

Each warder knew his Span. Perhaps there was a span allocation roster or perhaps they drew lots. As the span name was called out by the yard warder going under the name of Suitcase van Rensberg, the relevant warder moved forward, stopped in front of the Head of the Prison, stamped each foot once vigorously on the ground keeping his arms straight down the side, kicked the right foot up to swing his body through ninety degrees in the horizontal plane and trampled down the yard and out the two gates as if going to war followed by the span. Each of the double fences had a gate.

I looked up and was intrigued to observe Napoleon Bonaparte himself complete with his right hand holding his heart but with a modern prison warder cap masquerading as the Chief Warder Theron, Head of the Robben Island Prison, standing at the gate acknowledging each warder's foot stamping routine and glaring at each Work Span as they passed by. What amused me more was that in the Bo-Kaap where I grew up there was also a Napoleon

Bonaparte shortened to Japolean to fit the language of the Bo-Kaap, but he was a mental patient who walked around like Napoleon with a row of medals on his chest to the amusement of the whole neighbourhood. The Napoleon of the Bo-Kaap could not really be called the 'village idiot' because he was much loved by the people of the area. This 'Japolean' of Robben Island was a world apart.

On the other side of the yard stood Head Warder Zeelie glaring at each prisoner with his beady eyes and restlessly swinging his right leg as if wanting to kick each prisoner as he passed. Zeelie never carried a baton or pick axe handle. His weapon of choice was the foot. This earned him the nickname "The Ostrich" amongst the prisoners or "Volstruis" in Afrikaans amongst his fellow warders. Kicking was supposed to be the ostrich's mode of attack. Even Chief Warder Theron once asked him if he was an ostrich when he saw him kick a prisoner who accidentally stepped out of the line. To my amateur psychologist eye Zeelie looked seriously psychotic.

Ekwilbou was standing with the Bou Groep Span (Building Work Group) at the farthest corner of the yard waiting for his Span to be called by the yard warder. Comrade Makana who worked in the Bougroup told me that Ekwilbou's conversation in the early morning was always about how many bricks he wanted layed that day. He wanted a thousand bricks from each bricklayer. I remembered the industrial standard for bricklaying in Cape Town at that time was eight hundred per day. David Mmutle once told me that if one of the bricklayers should lay a brick not to his liking he would scream "Bêre daai blerrie baksteen reg!" (Save or hoard that blerry brick correctly).

What struck me also was that there were not too many rubber batons around. That to me implied that marks or injuries here did not matter. There was no court of law here to pretend to protect the weak.

Masendane ("He of the big crotch"), who came a few years later, was another source of amusement during morning work deployments as he trudged with gaping thighs at the head of his span of prisoners out of the two gates after his foot stamping routine in front of his Opper (as the Chief Warder was called by the prison staff).

The span followed their warders and the armed guards trailed further behind. If there was an officer present in the yard, recognizable by the brass buttons clipped on the shoulders boards on his shirt or jacket, the warders would go and do the foot stamping act in front of him as well but would also swing their right hand up to their forehead and down to the side just after the foot stamping act and before the ninety degree swing. The added hand to forehead swing of the arm performance was reserved for 'officers' only. This all was done just as my common law 'mentor' described the day before when he explained to me how the gang that he called the Big Six greeted one another. I surmised that the armed guard kept a safe distance from the procession lest he be attacked and his gun or rifle taken away by one or more of the dangerous mild mannered teachers or lawyers they were escorting to their place of hard labour.

Finally it was our turn, the Quarry Span, to get ready to march out and a ripple of movement passed along our ranks caused by a slight hesitation before stepping out. We were about seven hundred men standing in fours in the quarry line up. There seemed to be extra activity around the yard with increased tension and an air of trepidation evidenced by yet another ripple along the quarry queue. The Quarry Span was about to go. Finally the words "Quarry Span" pronounced "Gwarrie" with a heavy underlining was called out. The Quarry span was the last to leave since the 'dregs' of the labour force of Robben Island was condemned to the stone quarry. There was a lime quarry somewhere where Nelson Mandela and company worked but it did not have the reputation and awe of the stone quarry. I tried to look to the back to see how far the quarry span extended when I heard a commotion somewhere near the gate. I looked around the person in front of me and saw a prisoner been shoved and dragged by the collar and sleeve of his white canvass jacket by two warders towards the punishment cells, followed by another warder just in case an additional hand or baton was needed. I still remember that plaintive voice shouting, "Ek willie we-k -ie, ek sallie we-k -ie, ek gaan nie we-k -ie", dropping the r sound in the Afrikaans word "werk" and the n in the "nie". (I do not want to work, I will not work, I am not going to work) interspersed with "Ons gaan jou nou bliksim" ("We are now going to beat you"). Sambotla, who was standing next to me, explained that "Won't Work" was a common law prisoner who was fired from his very comfortable job in the Cleaners span and was now refusing to go to the quarry. He must have fallen out of favour or he was 'pimped" (the prison term for being informed on) and he would probably be assaulted (get a carry on) when he reached the hospital where his injuries would be roughly patched up and then this prisoner will be thrown into a punishment cell. Refusing to work, I later learnt, was a serious offence described as the ultimate of "lui en traag" (lazy and slothful). This epithet was also later, I should be ashamed to say, often 'affixed to my name' (to again use the terminology of the court warrant that brought me to Robben Island in the first place). The carry on was where the warders assaulted the prisoner in a free for all style hence the name 'Carry on'.

The culukoet (spoken with some apprehension) was the solitary confinement cells and I think that the term culukoet was somehow related to the "cooler" describing the same cold and bleak solitary confinement quarters in a different prison culture. Little did I then know how often I would be visiting that dreary place, sometimes bloodied by an assault, other times whole and with skin intact. Zambotla whispered to me that sometimes common law prisoners avoided going to the quarry by cutting the tendon of their foot just above the heel that then made it impossible for them to walk and hence work in the quarry. He had seen quite a number hobbling on one foot with the 'treated' foot flapping helplessly. This made me wonder what terrors the quarry held that common law prisoners tried to avoid it at such a cost. I would certainly know soon enough and that morning I could hardly wait to go and see for myself.

Chapter 5

Hard labour in the Quarry

After the third short delay it was the Quarry Span's turn to go through those fateful looking gates. Again the Yard Warder shouted "Gwarrie, stap uit!" and again underlined as before and we started moving like a fan unfolding. Four common law prisoners carrying a stainless steel drum between them lead the way to the 'Gwarrie'. After being counted we passed "Napoleon Boneparte" and then went through the gates with guards armed with Belgian FN automatic rifles trailing behind and to the sides of us and warders with batons or pick axe handles marched a bit nearer.

The track in which the Quarry prisoners walked soon descended into a type of uneven dug-out channel and only our heads and shoulders were above the surrounding ground level for most of the way across the Island to the infamous quarry. The warders and guards armed with their rifles thus walked on the higher ground beside the channel, which made them seem even more threatening. This channel was later filled in and replaced with a blue stone gravel track and fenced with barbed wire on both sides as well as overhead forming a very long cage stretching from the prison across the Island to the stone quarry. I again wondered what then gave this group of mild mannered men working in the quarry such a dangerous reputation that it made it necessary for them to trudge all the way to their place of labour in a in a channel or a barbed wire cage. They were mostly students, teachers, lawyers, farmers, mine workers and youngsters. True there were a few trained guerrillas with us but they were in the minority. It was not difficult to determine where the need for security ended and plain malice started. The cage nevertheless made us feel a bit more secure since it effectively stopped assaults en route to the quarry.

A hulk of a man with smallish eyes, a bullish neck and an angry red face came galloping by on horseback. Zambotla, who was walking next to me, whispered that that was Sergeant Delport, the Head (and terror) of the quarry fittingly nicknamed 'LeBomvu' meaning the "Red One" and I saw the common law prisoners walking with us look at him with awe. He was, according to Zambotla and others, a mean and cruel man who thought nothing of taking a gun and shooting down a prisoner he disliked and then reporting that the prisoner tried to escape and crossed the dead line. He was also known to take prisoners to the tool shed for private beatings. I was seriously advised to keep out of his way. We trudged on in heavy silence with the warders occasionally shouting at us to keep quiet. In the intermittent silence along the road to the 'Gwarrie' I started wondering what warder training was like. Like a lecturer having to learn elocution, warders must attend courses in practical shouting (Yelling 101) besides the pick axe handling course.

Eventually we reached the quarry to be counted once more just in case somebody disappeared out of the cage along the way. The quarry air had the invigorating smell of the sea reminding me of picnicking on the beaches of Cape Town and I suffered a brief spell of nostalgia that I hastily suppressed. Today, even after so many years, that same sea smell still reminds me, not of holiday and fun any more but rather of prison and that awful quarry on Robben Island.

The quarry itself was a large enclave with a blue slate stone outcrop a little lower down. The outcrop must have been cleared earlier after much digging through layers of top soil and sea sand. A petrol driven pump to control seawater seepage into the mining area had been installed right from the beginning. A barbed wire fence surrounded the whole quarry. Just outside the quarry a crop of wild flowers could be seen. Even God's goodly flowers seemed to have avoided that quarry. The sea was visible on the other side of a semi-encircling pathway held up with a sand and stone dune. This pathway eventually became a road and the sand dune a dyke from the many loads of stone and sand we wheel-barrowed, struggling up that path to dump into the sea or on that dune. On one side of the Quarry near to the gate that trucks used to enter and leave the quarry, was a huge hill of blue stone gravel flattened on top – the end product of the stone crushing labour group known as the "Nap Liners". It was, in fact one of the end products of the whole production line. I later came to know from first-hand how much sweat and pain went into that dyke and into that hill of blue stone gravel.

Zambotla told me that the "Graaf Span" (spade work group) was the easiest since prisoners classified as light labour by the doctor were often assigned to this work group. I then made my way to the queue where spades were been issued by one of the common law 'Quarry Attendants' especially appointed by Delport from amongst his Big Fives. Standing amongst the sickly and infirm I felt as if I was masquerading as a light labourer but as a novice I can, in fact, claim to be a light labourer. The other work groups to choose from included the pick-axe span, wheel barrow drivers, the big hammer swingers, the nap liners, the rope span, and the wall/dyke builders and later the stone dressers. The most privileged worker was Delport's coffee maker. This job was occupied by a criminal and high ranking Big Five member (a so-called pimp) responding to the name Dum-dum. I wondered if this had anything to do with the dum-dum bullet the South African police were then starting to use against demonstrators. These bullets were illegal in terms of International law since it tumbles in flight and can cause extensive injuries. In the Quarry his job title was at the very lofty prisoner rank known as an "Agterryer", that seemed to be at the level of authority just below warder (legal or not) and opened exclusively to properly 'qualified' and properly connected common law prisoners. Next in line in this hierarchy was a Big Five gang member called "Fynkyk" which approximately translates into "fine observer". His self-appointed job was thus to watch out for lazy prisoners and other evil doers who dared to infringe quarry and prison rules.

The wheel barrow span, Zambotla informed me, was freer because there was no one warder to supervise and watch the 'work' but the work was tough and arduous. Two types of wheelbarrows were available: some were of the de lux variety with pneumatic rubber wheels and others with iron wheels. Iron wheeled wheel barrows were issued to prisoners Delport did not like simply because an iron wheelbarrow was much harder to push especially through sand and particularly if the wheelbarrow axel was rusted and dry. Members of this fortunate 'cast', specially selected and duly 'appointed' by Delport, could be heard from a distance grunting and iron wheels squeaking along always accompanied by raucous shouts from the warders urging the wheelbarrows (not the drivers) to move faster and reminding the drivers that the wheelbarrows are not tired. One of Delport's favourite jokes is to ask new comers if they have driver's licenses and then to find great amusement in the change of expression when the aspirant lorry drivers are issued with wheel barrows.

The Nap Line where prisoners sat in rows breaking stones into gravel with four pound hammers was bad because at the end of the day the amount of gravel produced was measured and if you did not produce enough concrete stone of the correct size then your ticket would 'fly' (i.e. be taken by a warder) and you would be charged with being lazy (lui en traag). This work group I was advised to avoid until I gained more quarry experience.

There was also a type of figurative 'block' in the quarry and the 'temperature' of this 'block' was a measure of condition, atmosphere or level of tension in the quarry that day. If the block was hot then the condition in the quarry was bad and it often meant that Delport had gone crazy and was harassing prisoners as well as warders, who in turn would harass prisoners who would then bear the brunt of assaults and other forms of meanness. There was also a similar 'block' in the Yard and when that 'block' was hot then the cleaners would 'fly' that is they were sacked and sent to the quarry. There might also be searches of the cells and prisoners would be up on charges of being in possession of contraband or "Unauthorized articles". I must, with a bit of shame, say that sometimes I was, by the projects I had, the cause of the block getting hot during my term there. It can therefore be understood why prisoners always enquired about the condition of the 'block'. "How is the 'block' in the Quarry?" or "How is the 'block' in the Yard?" If the 'block' was hot in the yard then you needed to hide your contraband and other illicit articles and newspaper cuttings. The common law prisoners taught us the usage of this idiom. I later learnt that the origin of this proverbial block was a metaphor from the motorcar engine block. If this block gets hot, probably as a result of driving the car without oil as a result of a leaking sump or water as a result of a leaking radiator or cylinder head gasket, then the engine would get hot and be in danger of cracking and this would then mean huge problems for the owner of the car. It is a really a reflection of the types of cars working class people own.

Following Zambotla's advice I went to stand in the spades queue but Delport, who happened to pass, tapped me on the shoulder and growled that I must leave the spades and select a pic- axe and go to the Pick-axe group. He grumbled about wanting to see how I worked and 'what I was made of'. Wondering what that could mean I reluctantly left Zambotla in the spades queue and joined the group collecting pick axes. I looked around and there was Zambotla getting a pick-axe as well. He was taking his role as mentor very seriously. With pick axes hoisted over our shoulders we bravely marched out to join Mgabela, Bolente, Bolise, Makaleni, Zuma, Wusi and others of the pick-axe group and together we went off to what appeared to be a wide shallow trench in the higher area of the quarry. We formed a long double row in font of another line of prisoners with spades. This seemed to me to be a type of an alluvial stone mine – not the blue stone variety found further down the quarry but the earthy brown type. This field was to be cleared of stones to a depth of about one metre as if the area would become a crop-producing field. I believe that, just as in the Landbou group, the Agricultural theory was that if the stones could be removed then ploughs could be used without any danger to their blades and also the roots of the crop could grow free without obstructions and hence the field would be more productive. Productivity was after all the key issue in the Quarry.

There was a warder standing at the front of the shallow trench and we had hardly arrived when he bellowed "Kom gaan aan met julle werk! Waarom staan julle so rond! Jy sal jou kaartjie verloor" (Come get started with your work. Why are you standing around, you will lose your ticket). It seemed that there was some great urgency with this work as with all work in the quarry. It was as if a delay would cause us to miss the pre-ordered rain and the growing season with our unprepared field, or the quarry would fail to reach some quota of stones production. We, the pick axe span, having lined up lifted our pick axes and swung them down into the ground together with a unanimous grunt except that I missed the unanimity and my pick axe fell to (I could not say bit into) the ground a little later to topple over in the sand. It must be remembered that this was absolutely the first time I had ever had a pick axe in my hand. I do not remember ever seeing a pick-axe in my former life and I had to learn the mechanism of the process of pick axing. Then Mgabela broke into a song. I still remember that song having heard it thousands of times during my years of forced labour in the quarry. Everybody in the Span joined in the song, except me, simply because I could not sing never mind I didn't know the words. The song had a deep African Rhythm and the lead singer singing at a higher octave wove a melody into the basic rhythm. Although I did not understood its meaning then, the tone was mournful and full of yearning yet with a strong element of hope. It reminded me a little, not so much the music but the emotion of Dvorak's New World.

> *Sikhulumu ngeNgqause ekuseni madoda,*
> *Hausa sabelabe sajho.*

And the lead singer brought in the words: " *E-Pitoli, enew loko*"
And we, the chorus, joined in with *Ullale lamdana* –
And the lead singer would join in with *ifune pimp abelungu*
And we, the chorus would add *"Hausa sabelabe sajho*
Followed by the lead singer's mournful " *ekuseni, ekuseni madoda, ekuseni mfwetu"*

And the pick axes dropped and bit into the ground to be lifted again with "Huasa sabelabe sajho." The sound became almost hypnotic and the 'labour' lightened a bit for me. As the ground was loosened we moved forward and some of the spades followed us a short distance behind digging out stones from the loosened earth. The stones were carried to the back of the stone mine by the stone carriers who were mostly the more privileged common law prisoners (since this was lighter labour) to be piled up behind the spade span, some to be taken away by political prisoners pushing wheel barrows to dump into the sea and others to be used to construct terrace walls. The stones for the terraces were generally smaller since the larger stones were to be carted away by the wheel barrows and must, out of spite, provide enough weight for the wheel barrows, or that was what I thought.

The terrace walls were being built about half a meter high a little distance from where we were digging and backfilled with soil by the other half of the Spade Span walking endlessly to and fro with spades of soil.   In my mind's eye I looked into the future across these terraced fields and saw maize growing at one level and beans at another and millet at the lower except that there was no water for irrigation on this barren Island and these terraces we were constructing with so much sweat and pain would remain barren. It was all make-believe farming there in that arid stone quarry.   Nothing grew in that Godforsaken Quarry except weeds. I thought that nothing wanted to grow there but during winter a fragrant wild herb (that we prisoners called mhliguyani) found its way inside the Quarry fence to sooth our bronchitis and blocked noses during the strenuous winter cold.

Years later after I went to look for these terraces and found none. All our hard work had been obliterated.

The 'Landbou' (Agriculture) Span was somewhere towards the centre of the Island under the control of sub-humans posing as warders that included the Kleynhans brothers.   They were also building terraces for 'farming'. There, prisoners who were accused of 'laziness' were handcuffed and buried up to their necks in the blazing sun and no one dared to ask for water when the heat became too much since the only water they could expect was piss served on the complaining heads directly from the Kleynhans' "kidney wiper" to use the terminology from Eddy Daniel's famous song.

A warder nicknamed Hodoshe, a short squat man was in charge of and haunted the Terrace Construction Span in the Quarry and he enjoyed walking up and down the terraces with arms hanging wide growling at and pestering prisoners as befitted his nickname that meant the 'green fly', an insect that is well known for its cussed peskiness. He was very proud of that name believing it meant "strong man". He certainly lived up to his name as the Green Fly with his constant nagging to make the terrace constructors work faster. Some common law prisoners also worked on the terraces but they were there to support the Green Fly. They selected and packed the stones that formed the terrace walls. This was work for a higher caste and you needed to be 'elevated' to that level by Delport himself. The work of the even more privileged common law prisoners was to put what they called "chokers" into the walls of these terraces. Chokers were smaller stones inserted into holes or gaps in the terrace walls that the terrace builders overlooked or could not manage with the supply of larger stones at their disposal. It was thus regarded as highly specialised work.

The work with the pick axes was tiring but the songs kept me going until Delport arrived for inspection. I then had the opportunity to examine Delport more closely. He seemed to be in his late thirties or early forties. He had a permanent grin that became more mirthless when malice increased. What struck me about Delport now that I was able to examine him from a closer range were his eyes, thick neck and his red angry face. The smallish eyes seem to lack something that would have distinguished them from the eyes of an animal. I imagined they lacked that glimmer which could have made them human. A number of warders seemed to have the same look but with Delport the condition was more acute. Delport stood looking at us for some time and then stopped the song of the pick axes with an angry bark and growled that the current song was not a fitting song for the 'Amper Baas'. He seemed to have a bit of problem with his speech, which quickly transformed into a bark or growl when words could not come out. With some sense of paranoia I had the queer feeling that the name Amper Baas was referring to me. He wanted a faster song – the Zip song he said was what he wanted. Now, reluctantly, the song became

Tjhona pick,.. tjhona pick ... Zip!

> *Tjhona pick... TJhona pick ... Zip!*
> *Tjhona pick... Tjhona pick ... Zip!*

Tjhona means "down" and I supposed referred to the pick-axes since with the two "Tjhona picks", the pick-axe was lifted and swung to bite into the soil in time with the Zip to be again quickly lifted with more Tjhona picks all under the baleful glare of Delport. A quick breather was taken after a round of three hurried tjhona pick zips with the words by the lead singer

> *Abelung,.... God damn, ...God damned... God Damned*

(Whiteman, God damn you and the second and fourth God damn repeated by us, the chorus like an echo). This was then the resting phase. Sometimes the God damned was repeated again to provide an additional rest period and I felt that this was especially introduced into the song for me, the novice. And then the tiring 'tjhona pick zip' part started all over again. I was soon so exhausted that I could hardly lift the pickaxe just letting it drop under gravity each time, often missing the rhythm altogether then had to resort to a clumsy private tjhona pick zip on my own. When the lead singer noticed this he would slow down for me to catch up. By that time it was blazing hot; the sun having dried up and dispersed the morning cool.

Sometimes by late morning, if Delport felt a bit kind (i.e. when the 'block' was cool), the common law water carriers were allowed to come along with a pail of brackish water. That day they did come and this gave us, and particularly me, (the new comer) a brief respite. After the drink Delport stood watching us for sometime lifting and swinging our tjhona picks. I heard him swear under his breath, loudly declared the "Amper Baas" useless ("goed vir niks") and instructed a warder to take my prison identity card. He wanted to see me put me up on a charge of having been lazy (he called it "lui en traag") because, it seemed, I did not swing the pickaxe with enough zeal. Perhaps he expected more enthusiasm from me for his 'agriculture' project there in that barren Stone Quarry. Delport finally left and the change of the labour songs to a more sedate rhythm brought a bit of relief. The words of the song to me sounded now like

Oja khalo Ju-Ju

Before he left Delport told the warder that he must see to it that the Amper Baas joined the wheel barrow span for the afternoon. "Sien dat hy 'n yster wiel kry" (See that he gets an iron wheel) Delport yelled as he left. I was to discover what this meant. Luckily the bell rang for lunch which also stopped me wondering what an "yster wiel" could be.

We were counted and herded into a wire-mesh enclosure that looked like a paddock complete with a broken asbestos trough of muddied water in the middle. At the entrance gate each prisoner was given a much dented metal plate with either a handful of maize kernels still in cellulose jackets or white maize grit with a boiled onion on top – depending on the colour of one's skin. I was too exhausted to eat and there were blisters on my hands. My mouth was dry and the maize grit in any case had a bland taste the flavour and texture of cotton wool and because my mouth was so dry I could not swallow. Anger and frustration was another set of emotions I had to control. Zambotla came, looked at me with concern and fed me some of his puza mandla, a drink made from maize powder on the diet scale of prisoners with black skins. The irony of the name of this drink completely missed me. I later learnt that Puza mandla meant a sip of strength. I laid there in the sand and gravel trying hard to recover. The half hour lunch break seemed like five minutes. Delport came out of his office, a rough jerry built Wendy house next to our paddock, and yelled to us to fall in and I thought fall in was really an apt word to describe my physical condition that day. A bell was rung and I dragged myself to the pick-axe span but the warder remembered and took me to fetch a wheel barrow from the store.

I now became a proud driver of a wheelbarrow with an iron wheel. I joined the endless row of wheelbarrow drivers who collected stones at one end of the quarry, which the pick axe and the spade spans were mining out of the earth, and dropped into the sea at the other end of the quarry. To-and-fro in the hot afternoon sun I struggled and pushed that blessed wheelbarrow. From above we must have looked like the endless row of ants crawling from one end of the quarry to the dyke and back except that in the activity of ants there was an element of productivity. As Zambotla said, there was no warder in charge of the wheelbarrow span and that was a boon but all along the route the wheelbarrow pushers were egged on by warders guarding other spans with shouts of "Stap uit" (step out meaning push faster) or "move it", "daardie kruiwa is nie moeg nie" (that wheelbarrow is not tired!)

The criminal, going by the name Dum-dum who I now knew as second in charge of the Quarry even tough his main job was carrying mugs of coffee to Delport throughout the day came past when I was having a breather. It seemed that his supplementary job in the quarry was watching political prisoners for when he saw me standing having a breather he immediately started to make a commotion shouting, jumping up and down and gesticulating wildly that here was a Poqo (me) "wat weier om te werk, kom kyk hier baas" (who was refusing to work, come and see master) and the plump Warder Meintjies dutifully responded and came rushing to demand my identity card so that he could charge me for being "lui en traag" (lazy and slow). Fynkyk also arrived to inspect me with his beady eye. But my card was already taken. I was already up on a charge of laziness that morning arising out of my work performance with the pick-axes. There was then only one stone in my wheelbarrow and a rather smallish stone to boot. I found the fat round face of Meintjies glaring at me with disgust. I was told that my wheel barrow better be full of stones or else "gaan jy jou gat sien vanaand" (You will see your arse to-night). This was a popular warder threat but I never learnt what hole ("gat") was been referred to. It could have meant that you will see your grave or it could refer to your arse). Meintjies personally escorted me to the stone 'mine' to demand that the common law prisoners who were doing the loading put enough stones in my wheel barrow each time I came around otherwise they too would see their 'gat' tonight. Pushing an iron wheel wheelbarrow through the sand was hard work and the extra load of stones made the struggle even more difficult. My muscles, unaccustomed to so much labour, ached and the blisters on my hands were frayed through and oozing blood. The size six shoe on my left foot hurt and the size nine shoe on my right foot had a blister from sliding up and down as I trudge along. The uphill stretch of sandy ground was the toughest part of the journey. I was half way through the sandy leg of my journey up to the embankment along the sea when through that brain blistering heat and haze of sweat I saw Zambotla coming up with a rubber wheeled wheel barrow for me with the complements of comrade Nontente Kamteni who would take over the iron wheel. He told me to stop at the blacksmith's shed where he had organized some lubricant for the wheel. After the exchange of wheelbarrows and the oil I felt like I was now driving a Mercedes Benz and I understood the malice of Delport when he wanted me to have an iron wheeled wheelbarrow even though there were still some wheelbarrows with pneumatic rubber wheels left in the tool store. I still think with gratitude of my comrades in the quarry who tried hard to make my transition to prison life and hard labour easier despite them actually having greater and more serious problems than I. I realized that I still did not know what Zambotla's sentence was.

As the days passed I gradually got used to the hard labour in the stone quarry. The blisters on my hands gradually changed to calluses and my muscles became smaller and harder. I lost a bit of weight as we all did. The watery porridge with the pink streaks in the morning and the handful of boiled maize chips or grain with the insipid boil onion for lunch was too meagre to support the heavy labour. Ultimately it was not the hard physical activity or endless nagging, violence and threats from the sub humans of that quarry that was the greatest cause of anguish, nor was it the heat that made me wonder if perdition there in the underworld where sinners must all go could be worse. It was rather the sheer uselessness of our activity that came to pain me most What we did in that quarry cannot be called work or labour since work implies productivity and labour is a creative human activity and the very basis of existence. I once told the Head of the Prison that I had been sentenced to hard labour and I had not done a stitch of labour yet. He wanted to know what I did in the quarry every day and why I had not been charged with refusing to work. He reminded me that if he heard that I was refusing to work then I would see my 'gat'. The discussion that followed was fruitless but I think I came to know what is to be a slave with the complete loss of self actional identity. In the quarry permission was required to even visit the toilet bucket or to be allowed to 'wipe your kidney' into the wind.

Some of us found adaptation easier, I had initial difficulties adapting to the hard labour and the tedium, but for others it was even worse. For example comrade S tried to give up and went to the guard post to demand to be rather shot and killed right there. I still remembered the mocking laughter from the guard: "Ek gaan jou nie 'kill' nie, die gwarrie gaan jou 'kill', the kruiwa en the groot hammers gaan jou 'kill'. (I am not going to kill you, the quarry will kill you, the wheel barrows and the big hammers will kill you).

As I adapted to the physical effort there in that quarry the soul destroying tedium of the labour seemed to increase. I fought this as best as I could. Wheelbarrow work was particularly lonely. Eventually I learnt to switch my mind out from that quarry and think of other things. Walking around with my mind somewhere else became a habit. Pushing and struggling with wheelbarrow up and down the inclines and through the sand became an automatic type of reflex of which I was hardly conscious. I still today involuntarily go into this mode and may pass friends or acquaintances looking at them but not seeing them.

I had ample opportunity during subsequent days as I walked along with my wheelbarrow to study the security arrangements as well as the general layout of the quarry. There were four two metre high lookout posts for guards armed with Belgian automatic rifles. That was the time before South Africa made its own automatic rifles. These guns were, I believed, also called Sten guns and seventy year old Louis Tukani from Rural Transkei, having looked at these guards standing up there with these guns and doing nothing, thought and later started referring to these guns as "standing guns" perhaps in analogy to walking sticks – a stick for walking and a gun for standing.

The single row two-metre high barbed wire fence that surrounded the quarry was of poor quality and appeared not too difficult to negotiate under. The guards were not particularly attentive with their 'standing guns' especially by late afternoon since nobody was expected to attempt to escape. The sea with its sharks must have been regarded as sufficient deterrent. It was a boring job there on the guard posts but I must remember that the minds of warders are either trained or naturally attuned to such boring work. Later we did occasionally dodge out through a hole in the fence, never mind the deadline, not to escape but to forage for newspapers. This also gave me a chance to admire the incongruent looking bunches of wild flowers growing beyond the fence. No flowers dare grow inside the quarry fence.

From the wheelbarrow route I was assigned to I was also able to observe and study the general "production" layout of the stone quarry. The words of the mission statement of the quarry as propounded by Ngusa also known as Chief Warder Coetzee (who came later) came to mind: "Daar in die gwarrie maak jy groot klippe klein en klein klippe fyn" (there in the quarry you will make big stones small and small stones tiny (i.e. into gravel).

The stone became the focal point, the be all and end all of our existence. We literally ate, worked, dreamt and lived stones and more stones. We did our studies on stones in the form of slates and we used stones to teach Arithmetic, used stones in our indoor games of Ludo or "Snakes and Ladders". There were stones in our food and our living quarters were made of stone. The whole quarry was a hive of activity centered around stones as if huge profits were dependent on extreme diligence with these stones. The only people not working were the warders but somehow to us they ceased to be thought of as people.

Further down and at a lower level was a huge blue stone cavity like a festering sore in the earth and which constituted the heart of the quarry. This was the labour area of the 14-pound sledge hammer span hammering away at chisels embedded in the blue stone cliff edge. This work span consisted of about five teams each of two bare chested prisoners each team member hitting away at the same chisel in alternate turns their sweat drenched muscles flexing and quivering in the bright sun light. Further along three or four prisoners with pneumatic drills were busy noisily drilling holes in a straight line along the blue stone cliff in which the wedge shaped chisels were placed in readiness for the big hammer teams to pound into the rock hoping to crack off a slab of stone. A chisel holder sometimes joined the big hammer team. His job was to hold the chisel steady using a long piece of stiff wire for the big hammer team to hit at. This seemed a dangerous job since he had to avoid stone splinters should a hammer miss the chisel. The roar of the heavy diesel engine rose and fell to satisfy the demands of the pneumatic drills for compressed air as it clattered and stopped and clattered. This and the metallic rattle of the drills were painful to the ears if you went too near.

Walking along with my wheelbarrow I watched the 14 pound hammers rising and falling each time producing a dull metallic thud until eventually a long crack formed which rapidly increased in size with each pound of the hammer and as the long chisel sank deeper into its hole and, for a short distance, I walked in unison with the hammer swingers - left, right; hammer one, hammer two. The dull thuds kept beat with the tempo of my walk. A massive slab of rock broke off from the main piece of outcrop and fell down with a subdued crash and slight tremor of the ground. A slab of stone had been successfully dislodged from the mother lode.

These Big Hammers were spoken of with awe because the big hammer gang was a special span manned in the earlier days by tough common law prisoners. They were not under too much pressure to work but all of them were well muscled which also made them formidable fighters in the cell brawls that occurred from time to time amongst the common law prisoners. The big hammers were the muscle developing apparatus of these fighters. Perhaps this explained their preference for weapons such as spades that could be swung like hammers at the heads of their opponents. This span was also entitled to rest at will without being harassed. Ernest Malgas from the ANC became a big hammer man quite early in his quarry career until he was promoted to coffee waiter for Delport when Dum-dum was transferred out of Robben Island. I think he was the first in a long line of effort to subdue Delport psychologically by trying to talk to him. Malgas tried to talk to Delport about what is a human whilst serving his coffee and Jeff Masemola and Tony Suze later took up this subject. I also like to think that I too added to the effort to humanize Delport.

A short distance from the hammer span was the 'ngala' span at a rank slightly below the Big Hammers. These prisoners handled huge steel crowbars, pointed at one end and flattened on the other each about two metres in length and six centimeters in diameter called 'ngalas. Their job (read punishment) was to pry out the cracks if the chisels of the big hammers went too deep without opening the crevasse and loosen a bolder from the cliff face in preference to using another chisel on top of the one that went too deep. They also used their ngalas to further pry open cracks and thus drop big slabs of stones from the rock face. Walking with my wheelbarrow high above the area where the stones were quarried I watched the ngala span grunting and flexing their muscles as they strained to widen the crack to break off yet another stone from the mother lode. My thoughts came to an abrupt end by the raucous voice of Head Warder Jordaan, better known as Beelzebub shouting at me to "stap uit" (step out i.e. move faster) or else my ticket would fly followed by a whole series of swear words. Jordaan was Delports relief when Delport was sick or went for gun practice or on leave. Jordaan had the rapid talking skill of a fisherwoman and had a large repertoire of expletives and swear words except that he could not say a word of it in English. One of the techniques to deflate Jordaan was to ask his pardon and to politely request him to repeat what he said explaining that he was talking to fast to understand. I sometimes gave in to the temptation to ask Jordaan to repeat himself in English, but I knew what his answer would be if I should start with "I beg your pardon Head warder, I could not understand what you just said. Please repeat yourself." His answer was always "Pardon se moer, ek sal jou aankla, ek sal jou opfok" (Pardon's mother, I will put you on charge, I will beat you up). I heard this 'pardon se moer' so often that it got stuck in my mind and even today whenever I hear somebody saying the word 'pardon', I cannot stop myself from silently adding "pardon se moer". I wonder what Psychologist would say about this.

After a slab of stone dropped to the bottom of the pit the rope span moved in. On my way back from where I dropped my load of stones into the sea I could see the rope being tied round a freshly quarried stone and strung out ahead and up the incline. The span made a double row with the stretched out rope lying on the ground between them. Each member of the rope span bent down simultaneously to pick up the rope and stood in readiness like a tug of war team with the Stone as the opponent. The stone must first be dragged out of the ditch and onto the smooth incline leading up to the loading area or the stone dressers' work place.

Some of the good stones were dressed (i.e. squared off using hammer and chisel) and taken away to be used for building the prison, the Kramat or other buildings on the Island by head warder Ekwilbou and his span. The rope span also made use of work songs. The extra effort required to pull the stone out of the ditch required a special and more powerful song or chant. I heard this chant starting off first softly like a mantra repeated over and over slowly increasing in volume and urgency.

ESandla… funin dau… funindau…

eSandla… funindau … funindau,

 A work spirit is being invoked. It is actually a call for hands (eSandla means hands) to help with the job in hand. In a free society those who felt like helping would step forward in response to the call for hands but here everybody in the span was compelled to step in or else be charged with being lazy (the eternal "lui en traag").   The words then changed to

ESandla… genalap… genalap

This was the prelude where everyone clutching the rope prepared his mind and muscle for the huge effort to follow in perfect unison, for only then can individual effort be minimized. The tempo and volume of the chant increased as each one revved up his muscles for the effort to follow, each prisoner in the group quietly murmuring "funindawo, ... genalap" echoing the leader. The tempo of the chant increased further and so did the volume to a peak and when the lead singer judged that every body was ready and the rhythm steady he abruptly changed the chant to the grunting

En sukinsu ku! ... En sukinsu ku! En sukinsu ku!

Effort was applied with each *ku*. It seemed as if the "*ku*" had a special magic endowing the span with superhuman strength. And when the stone came out of the ditch and landed on the level ground before the incline, a grunt of satisfaction was emitted by all who helped ending with

"*Koko moya*"

(meaning take a breather) and a brief well earned rest before Delport who happened to pass, shouted to remind the span: "daai tou is nie moeg nie ... daai tou word nie aangekla nie!" (that rope is not tired ... the rope will not be put on charge). That word iSandla became very special to us. It became a request for help under very diverse circumstances. Somebody struggling with a Mathematics or English problem during study time would call out 'Hey, iSandla.'

I also worked in this rope span and sometimes we had to lift out the stone without the help of a rope but with bare hands and sometimes, assisted by a crowbar or an ngala Span and the iSandla mantra would at each occasion be invoked. Now, after twenty years whenever I lift something particularly heavy at home or in my garden, I cannot help saying to my self

"*iSandla funin dau... funin dau... sandal,,, funin dau*",

even if there is nobody there.

The Rope Span then had to drag the stone further up the incline. The song leader started a song similar to the pickaxe songs and the stone was dragged rhythmically up the incline with pulses of effort exerted in unison whenever the song reached the point when energy must be applied. The rhythm and action was thus similar to pick-axing with the pickaxe drop replaced by the tug on the rope. This was to ensure that everyone in the span pulled together and also to make the tedious work more bearable. Sometimes, when the terrain through which the stone needed to be dragged was too rough, short poles used as rollers were slipped under the stone to assist as the stone was dragged along. This reminded me a bit of the method used by the slave builders of the Pyramids to move the huge blocks along. Steven Tshwete was often the lead singer for the rope span and the musical and dance improvisations he added was quite amusing; but nobody was better in lead singing than Malcomess Konditi affectionately known as Mgabela, who would provide excellent entertainment during the "work" with light footed dance at the rope end or with a very fancy swing and twirl of the pick axe when he was the lead singer of that span. Makaleni was another good lead singer. He was after all an expert in the African Dance known as the 'iXhlentsah".

I looked down at the rope span as I trudged along with my wheelbarrow. From a distance I heard the mournful song from the Rope Span as they dragged a huge stone along the ground:

Oja Khala Ju-Ju

about Ju-Ju who was in prison and crying bitterly.

The advantage of working in the rope span was that there were extended periods of idleness and rest when the rope was being tied around the stone. The help of the Ngala Span to lift the stone so that the rope could be slipped and tied under and around the stone was often called which meant another few precious moments of idleness and rest. Rest was a precious commodity to grab whenever possible. Sometimes the rope would slip out then there would be more periods of precious idleness. One of the labour saving tricks was thus to tie the stone with a knot in such a way that would slip out after a while or after a few pulls giving the span yet another rest. There were various levels of expertise in the art of resting in the hard labour quarry without picking up a charge of "lui en traag" and I learnt some.

On the higher side of the quarry was the nap line. Each nap liner had a piece of wire gauze stitched into softer brown material shaped as a pair of spectacles tied around the eyes with a string making each nap liner look like the comic hero Spiderman. This was said to protect the eyes against flying stone chips and never mind the face. Each prisoner on the Nap line sat on a stone with a slightly larger flat stone serving as a work surface at a slightly lower level in front of him. A stone was taken from a supply of stone chunks, placed on the work surface, held there with a rubber loop made from an old motorcar tire and pounded with a four-pound hammer. When the stone has been pulverized into smaller pieces (about centimetre in size) it was swept off the work surface to a space in the front using the rubber loop. A fresh stone was placed on the work surface to be pounded into gravel and swept off the front and so it went on the whole goodly day with the pile of crushed stones steadily increasing in volume.

There is, so the experts told me, a special technique for breaking the stone chunk. Never hit the stone across the grain unless it is thin enough. Always hit the stone from one side and along the grain. It will then split easily into thinner strips that can be broken into the required centimetre chips. Do not use stones which are multi-grains because they will be harder. Throw this aside or give it to the more experienced Nap-liners.

Three or four wheelbarrow pushers were constantly on duty to keep up the supply of stone chunks for the nap liners. Initially these were common law prisoners and they considered it their duty to also keep a look out for candidates for the "Lui en Traag" charge.

Each Nap liner had a half a 44 gallon drum of chipped stones to produce as a target before the day ended or else be charged with the ridiculous indictment of been lazy and slack (the eternal "Lui and traag"). There was something in the Labour Law about piecework not being legal and we insisted that measuring gravel output on the Nap Line was against this labour law. We eventually won this in court to the great chagrin of Delport.

The area around the nap line was generally quiet except for the monotonous clacking of the four-pound hammers occasionally in unison and most of the time in various phases of disharmony. Sometimes, if you waited long enough there might be a sudden simultaneous lull - a weird moment of silence that could last for just a second or so when every hammer was by chance in the lifted position. These moments of silence intrigued me greatly.

The saying then was that an angel must have then passed by the Nap line. The sounds of the Nap line thus made me think of mathematical sequences and stochastic processes. There was no singing here on the nap line. Every prisoner was sullenly engrossed in his own thought, estimating his rate of production and whether he would make the quota at the end of the dreary day. But as the comrades became more adept at napping stones conversation started even though the Nap line warders tried to suppress it. The Napline also became a good place to discuss Academic topics or political principles.

Measuring the amount of stones using a 44 gallon drum was cumbersome and time consuming. This was replaced by one of Delport's inventions. A stone measuring scale was constructed. This was a large wooden cross made by the blacksmith to Delport's specification. The cone shaped heap of stones produced for the day had to completely fill the space between the left or right horizontal and the upright of the cross when placed over the pile of stones produced by each Nap line prisoner. The cross was adjusted and became a fairly accurate estimate of the volume of half a 44 gallon drum. If the cone of stones did not completely fill or overflow the quarter cross then the prisoner was charged with the ever ready "lui en traag" and spent the next Sabbath in a cell in the Zinc section without food for forty eight hours. A wooden V would have worked but Delport specified a cross. The alternate significance of this cross and the Sabbath was, however, completely lost to Delport whom I later discovered was a religious man in his own narrow way.

After a day's work the Nap liners could be recognized from amongst the crowd by a self-massaging reflex of the back or the flicking of fingers to reduce the cramps in the right hand and arm or the slapping of fine stone dust from their clothing.

Later that year I found myself on that same blessed nap line by Delports personal invitation, hammering away at the blue slate stones. I could never make the quota of Delport's cross and often thought of dogging into Delport's store and cutting off a few centimetres from the legs of that tyrannous piece of wood. Fortunately there were comrades who became so expert at crushing stones that they could fill their quota before the end of the day and they were then able to crush extra stones to help me, and other incompetents, by topping up our measure of stones from their supply. Sometimes they produced more than required and then we actually had extra crushed stones in reserve. Klaas Mashisi, who was another incompetent academic, and I would store these stones in our 'stone bank' (a hole dug in the ground) when the warder of the nap line was not looking, ready for a 'rainy day'. This often saved our tickets when our comrades were unable to smuggle a supply of stones to augment our meagre amounts or when these expert stone crushers were absent from the Nap Line having been redeployed elsewhere in the quarry.

During the winter, out of pure malice, more prisoners were sent to the nap line so that they could be deprived of an opportunity to warm themselves with active 'work' on wheelbarrows or spades etc. Active work was kept for summer so that we could sweat our guts out in the hot sun. During winter the nap line was shifted higher onto the embankment. The idea was to maximally expose Nap liners to the icy North Westerly wind as it swept across the Atlantic. This wind, picked up damp spray as it crossed the Atlantic and was especially 'designed' to freeze the unfortunate Nap liners to the bone to realize Delport's promise that "jy gaan jou gat opvries vandag" (you are going to freeze up your arse today). The pain brought about by unrelenting cold, as opposed to the pain of physical injury, seemed to have entrenched itself in my memory since I still, up to this day, try to avoid cold with a neurotic apprehension.

Loose pieces of zinc were sometimes found in the quarry and the resourceful would use these pieces to build shelters against the winter winds. Others built stone wind shelters from the surplus stones supplied for crushing. Stones and pieces of zinc and cardboard were limited and thus not all were able to build shelters there on that Nap line. Some may thus have better shelters than others and still others may not be able to find the material to build shelters at all. There were lengthy discussions about the ethics of seeking wind shelters since these were in short supply leading to the classical 'have and have not' situation that was so much discussed during our political meetings. The majority opinion was that if all of us could not build or find shelter then none must build shelters or seek shelter. We either suffered together or found relief together. Shelters we decided should be dismantled. We would then continue to lodge our complaints during the Saturday morning complaints and requests parade and during the inspection parade on Sunday mornings and try and communicate this problem to our lawyers. Our brotherhood was developing and the strong sense of sharing even our pain was evolving. Unfortunately not all of us shared this sentiment of sharing pain. Some, as pointed out in an earlier chronicle, continued to enjoy self constructed wind shelters perhaps not knowing the reason the majority appeared to comply with Delport's instruction to demolish all shelters.

Delport came to look at our differences and must have left happy in the knowledge that he had created a division amongst us. There was a suggestion that this division was on organisational lines and that one organisation defied Delport's instructions and was therefore braver. This was not so. We came from the same basic cross section of the population. We generally had the same altruistic motives. We dreamt of the future of South Africa together, even though our ideas of the method of change and governance of that future South Africa and the method of redistribution of the land after freedom differed. We were prepared to suffer for that future together and because of this there grew a bond between most of us that transcended party differences and this bond still exists today. We had similar weaknesses and strengths and it was a simple statistical fact that the party with the biggest number would have the largest absolute number of successes (such as academic achievements) and a larger number of problems. It took planned and sometimes unplanned or spontaneous team building efforts using sport, for example, to dilute party differences. This, however, is not to suggest that party differences were neutralized. Fortunately those who did not want to share our discomforts in the quarry were few and their numbers diminished as we developed our bonds and empathy with one another.

I later told Delport that if the flying stone chips should break my spectacles then I would write to my lawyer to institute a claim against him and the state. Surprisingly I was never deployed to the nap line again but Delport tried to get his own back at me. My 'duties' were changed to, as he then put it to "driving a 'wheel-less' wheelbarrow" ("kruiwa sonder 'n wiel" he called it) mysteriously known as a "little buck" ("bokkie"). He crudely promised me that here in his quarry he would see that I "poep van voor en agter". (fart from the back and the front). Sometimes Delport would be more lyrical and would graphically describe when and from what part of the anatomy these winds would come. The wheel-less wheelbarrow I had to 'push' consisted of a 44 gallon drum sliced in half fitted between two rusty steel tubes to be carried as a bier and I with Achmad Cassiem, the other "amper baas", had to toil up and down the quarry carrying this bokkie loaded with stones. Sometimes I was the wheel (walking in front) and sometimes he was. Perhaps our movement around the Quarry simulated the movement of a sick springbok and hence the name 'bokkie'. It was one of the heaviest labours in the quarry but we, nevertheless, had interesting discussions with this "bokkie" wedged as it were between us.

The first task the wheelbarrow drivers (with or without wheels) had for the day was to transport the finished product, the pride of the Nap line, into storage so that it could not be stolen by enterprising but incompetent Nap liners like Klaas Mashishi and Sedick Isaacs. This was wheel barrowed to the huge flat-topped hill of chipped stones roughly two-metres high on the edge of the quarry near the gate. The wheelbarrows had to mount this hill so that the wheelbarrow driver could empty his wheelbarrow right on the top and briefly watch as the napped stones cascaded down the sides. This usually required a preliminary run. For the drivers of wheel-less wheelbarrows this feat was particularly difficult since the preliminary run before ascending this hill was not very effective but perhaps a bit better than the iron wheeled wheelbarrow.

On the other side of this hill of napped stones were six prisoners who spent the day spading the stones through a large bird wire sieve to separate the bigger stones from the smaller ones before it was either trucked away for building or dumped into the sea. Achmad and I were once 'promoted' to this job.   This job was back breaking. After a day of this 'work' we had to trudge back to prison grey with the fine stone dust on our skin and embedded in our hair making us look prematurely grey and we would then cough up grey stone dust in the bathroom during the evenings or blow it out of our noses. Sometimes during late afternoons after a day of shovelling stones through this sieve Delport would come to mock us. The "amper base" he taunted, was now looking more white than him, overlooking the fact that he was actually more red than white. I think prisoners 'working' in this span were at real risk of Silicosis or some form of lung disease and I wondered if it contributed to my TB episode.

Another work area was the coco-pans. Here prisoners had to transport sand from one end of the quarry to another pushing the cocopan on its rickety rails. This activity did not, however, last too long.   The cocopan was derailed too often to provide consistent hard labour. A coco-pan rail became a useful source of material for one of my later master key- making projects.

The other shed besides Delport's and the tools store was that of the Blacksmith. The incumbent was not really a blacksmith but the job was to keep the chisels of the stone dressers sharp, the hammers, pickaxes and spades in order and the wheelbarrows in a state of repair. The blacksmith also stocked the Mercurochrome ointment in the event of injuries that occurred rather frequently in the quarry with the flying stone chips and rickety bridge ways across crevasses. A common law prisoner held this job until he was drafted to another prison with the other common law prisoners. It was then taken over by Japhta Masemola known as Bra Jeff. Bra Jeff was a very technically competent person. He knew for example how to cleanly split the top of a bottle to convert it into a drinking glass with the equipment he had in the quarry. He also knew how to make screw jacks and rafts as well as how to knit socks. He was the best 'socks mechanic' on the Island.

The rain sometimes brought respite from the cold in the Quarry but only when Delport considered that we were wet enough, and the likelihood of the rain stopping that day was low. By that time we would most likely be soaked to the skin. Then we would be herded into the paddock that had a bit of rain shelter on one side but not adequate wind breaks and we would then start freezing up in our damp canvass prison jackets and tattered prison jerseys. If we were lucky and the rain continued, we were issued with rain capes; short plastic cloaks that reached only as far as the hips. We would then have to run via the barbed wire cage through the rain back to the prison. There were, however, times when the dark clouds blocking the sun would refuse to provide the blessed rain and we would then freeze the whole grey day in that awful quarry.

Every afternoon at about five o'clock a bell would finally bring relief. This was called the 'Chaila' bell and, as Eddy used to say, "all good things come to an end", the 'labour' stopped and the tools were taken back to the sheds. Another day in the Quarry came to an end but with thousands of days still to come. The trick is never to think too far ahead.

During that first day in the quarry my muscles were already aching long before that goodly bell. I was stiff from all the 'work' and the blisters on my hands were oozing clear fluid. I also had the start of stomach cramps that would lead to diarrhoea possibly from the pink streaks (worms) in the porridge and to which I had not as yet developed a resistance. This diarrhoea was to further weaken my system during my early days and made this initial period in the quarry even harder.

After that first day and every day for the next eight years of hard and useless 'labour' we were marched back to the prison via the same dusty trench we came, each prisoner within his own private world of pain, fatigue and depression and for some bordering on ill health. I sometimes think that fragments of our spirit must still be lying around there in that quarry since so much effort, I think, was made to break us.

At the gate of the prison another dose of humiliation awaited us. Stepping into the prison yard each prisoner had to strip completely naked and stand in a queue clutching his clothes. This was imposed during summer or winter, rain of shine. The clothes were handed to a warder one item at a time that felt each item along its length and along the seams and then threw it a short distance behind him. Before stepping past to retrieve his clothes the prisoner had to submit to body inspection of each fossa. The tongue must be clicked to show that there was nothing hidden in the mouth. Next the arms had to be lifted and the legs spread to show that there was indeed nothing hidden there and finally the anus to be exposed to show that there was nothing there as well. This last action known as the tausa was too much and we were firm in our rule that everybody must refuse to submit to any such form of bodily inspection.

That night after my first day in the quarry I slept without hearing the "alles reg" (the alls well) from the guards on their watch towers when their officers passed by through the night. The haze of pain and fatigue was engulfed by sleep. But sleep was far too short.

Thus we went through the pains of the quarry. It is indeed fortunate that the human mind does not seem to retain the memory of pain otherwise, I think, child bearing and pregnancies would for example, not have been so popular. I have indeed learnt that if the human mind did experience raw pain it does not remember it and the aversion experienced for very long. I believe this since I had my share of pain there on Robben Island and I do not remember much of it except perhaps the human malice behind it. It seems, however, that the pain of freezing aggravated by the North West wind blowing over the sea that left the jaw so tight that shivering soon turns into a cramp when the exercise of hammering on the nap line did not provide the warmth of movement that shovelling stones or wheelbarrow driving could provide, did indeed carry over. Freezing, whilst lying naked in a solitary confinement cell with the north wind leaking in through the window, cannot also easily be forgotten. Even the languid sensation that came about before the convulsive flexing and extension of the back, thigh and calf muscles starts is remembered as very unpleasant. I have a phobia for cold. Perhaps this type of hypothermia set in quicker for us prisoners because nourishment was inadequate. The porridge or the maize chips contained more water then maize. I have not met anybody else, besides ex Robben Island bandiete with such a neurotic fear of the cold. Even today an ambient drop in temperature is accompanied with a corresponding rise in apprehension. Whilst studying in Germany years later I became very fearful of the oncoming German winter even though I knew it to be totally irrational.

The following day I woke stiff and sore and dreaded another day in the quarry. I was told by Delport to stay with the wheel-barrow span until such time that I "improve" and I did not try to imagine what "improve" meant.

Pushing that wheelbarrow became to be the labour of my days and as the days pass I gradually grew use to the hard labour but had great difficulty with the stifling tedium. I knew that I as well as we as a community had to conquer that Quarry or perish. We had problems for which a solution must be found and I feared that the longer we delay the more irreversible changes might become. A solution was found. Whether this solution is acceptable is for the reader to judge.

Fig 2. Breaking stones on the Napline

Chapter 6

Cell Life

The slamming shut of that cell door after a day of tedium and misery in the quarry was a huge relief. As first the steel gate (or grill) then the steel door was slammed shut and double locked. We, prisoners, somehow now felt secure and protected against the warders with their meanness and their brutality and noise. In the cell we were 'free' to do as we pleased. I think the cell itself became a "cocoon" and we felt 'safe' in the confines of that cell. I would then recall the words of the Security Police when they shoved me in that cell in Caledon Square that seemed so long ago: "Here you will have freedom of speech, freedom of movement". This peculiar sense of security in the cells of Robben Island could well be the reason why random cell searches for contraband ("ongeoorloofde artikels") were particularly disturbing and stressful even for those who had nothing to hide.

The warders would then intruded into our privacy and we resented them coming into our cell and scratching through our meagre personal possessions.

In the cell an atmosphere of brotherhood prevailed that grew stronger with time together and is difficult to describe. Cell members were very attentive to the needs of each other. Anybody who wished to address the cell on any issue merely had to clap his hands and he would be heard.   Attention was immediate.   Most of the times reasons for seeking the cell's attention was for lost articles or books.   Occasionally somebody would announce: "To-day, gentlemen I am 'cracking'".   Cracking was our term for the periodic state of depression and perhaps 'home sickness' that befell most if not all of us at some time. Most of the time it was not mentioned but we would know and try and approach the comrade who had suddenly become quiet to help alleviate the 'cracking." We seemed to take turns going through states of depression. We called it "crack" in the rather sinister connotation of breaking up but the tone of the word gradually changed meaning so that when I announced that I was cracking I would mean 'have a little patience with me, I am not myself today".   It was during these periods that the pain of imprisonment became worst. Whenever this happened we knew that there would be support in some form sometimes with encouragement, a bit of humour or just quiet non-verbal support and togetherness. It was initially surprising to me how tangible this silent togetherness could become. Sometimes a quiet 'walk about' the area of the yard (if this was possible at that instant) would help. The trick was to sense the type of support that would fit the person "cracking" and the mood of the moment.

The members of a cell were informally subdivided into what can best be called 'in- groups' – two or more comrades formed closer friendships within the cell, a form of "sub-family or closer brotherhood" group.   Such a group would share everything – soap, toiletries, stationery and even cell chores such as cleaning, polishing the floor or washing blankets during the weekends.

This group would also eat together. After my friend and mentor Sambodla was hanged Tony Suze, Lamek Kula and I formed such a group. I think this was the reason why the death of Lamek Kula later that year was particularly painful to me and why I so vividly remember the circumstances of his death and also the death of Zambodla. With Zambodla's death I went through a period of denial. I just could not get rid of the strong feeling or rather hope that he would come back and whenever a new group of prisoners came in I would look for his face amongst them irrational as it was.

I lived in C1 for the first seven years when I was not in the culukoet (the punishment cell). Cell C1 was the first official study cell. The lights there were brighter with external cream coloured glass fittings instead of the dim wired glass type standard in all other cells and there were desks along one wall - not desks to sit in front of "soos menere" (like misters) as the warders were inclined to say but to stand against to read, write or study as befitted prisoners ("soos dit bandiete betaam"). Luxuries like chairs and stools were not allowed (verbode). If you really wanted to sit when reading or studying then you had to roll your sleeping mat into a tube and stand it edge on next to the desk to form a crude and somewhat wobbly stool. It worked provided you did not sit with all your weight otherwise the makeshift stool would buckle under you. A belt woven from the nylon rope found on the shores by the Sea-Weed Span could be used to tie the tube chair to make it more stable.

We, nevertheless, wanted to see study facilities in all the cells and tried to register this in the weekend "Complaints and Request" Book as often as possible (just like with the football). Those who wanted to study were required to obtain formal permission from 'Pretoria' and the first requirement was that the applicants must have money in their account. Only Prison Department (Bureau of State Security) approved correspondence colleges and universities were allowed. The most popular institution was Rapid Results Correspondence College. We never used the other correspondence college trading under the name "Sukses" since we were inclined to believe that it was a Government college purely because it used Afrikaans as its media of instruction and lectures. The warders used this college when they too took up studying. The approved universities were the University of South Africa and the University of London.   Approval for the University of London was later withdrawn because 'Pretoria' thought that it might be a contact point with 'communists' and other such unsavoury characters who may have an adverse effect on our political development and consciousness.   The unstated definition of 'communist' then was anybody who disagreed with the South African Apartheid Government.

The Government's policy towards us was to isolate us from all political or suspected political news and events in the world. The theory seemed to be that this would help us to forget about our struggle and we would leave prison completely neutralized and thus 'reformed'. The policy of brutalizing us was, I think, geared to make the experience of prison as unpleasant as possible and thus make us not want to take part in any further political activities – a type of 'aversive therapy' or negative reinforcement. This, I think, was similar to the eighteen century philosophy of prison that gave rise to captions on prison doors such as "Let this be a place of dread to evil doers" replacing 'evil doers with 'Political Activists.' Only much later did they bring in a trained clinical psychologist at the rank of a colonel to, I think, analyse us. He tried hard to sell the concept of 'separate development' and the alienization of blacks in South Africa by the government creating a 'separate state' where they were supposed to be 'free'. Even in the animal world cats, this prison clinical psychologist would explain, prefer to live separate from for example lions and lions live separate from wolves. Apartheid can thus, he said, be regarded as a natural phenomenon. I spoke to him about what freedom was and I told him the story of my first arrest and how I was shoved into a six metre by three metre cell with the words that "In here you will be free – you will have freedom of speech and you can practice your politics to your heart's content. I also reminded him that black cats, grey cats and white cats do not notice the difference in their colours. I was at that time also studying psychology and when I first met this colonel it appeared that he was himself traumatized. He appeared very tense. I later heard that he had had a freak motorcar accident killing or seriously injuring the child of a fellow warder on the Island and that seemed to have troubled him greatly.

My first Christmas came and we were given a few days holiday from the quarry, the wash span, the building group etc. The intention was not really to give us a holiday but there was a shortage of staff during this period so that there were not enough warders and guards to take us out to the quarry. We also received our Christmas gift from the South African Prison Department – a mug of coffee made from the same brown sawdust as the daily morning coffee. Chief Warder Theron, condescending to speak English, came to wish us "a lucky Christmas" (which was his translation from the Afrikaans "gelukkige " which, in Afrikaans, could mean lucky or happy). Those who had money and who were allowed to buy a packet of biscuits and a packet of dried fruit or dates for Christmas received their orders. Indries Naidoo that year opted for dates instead of dried fruit. Unfortunately the dates did not arrive with the other orders so he went to complain and, in the spirit of Christmas, condescended to try Afrikaans saying " Mynneer, Ik het nogie my datums gekry" (Sir, I have not received my dates) and he was surprised when the warder, thinking Indries was asking after the date of his release said: "Koelie jy bly hier tot jy vrek" (Coolie, you stay here until you perish). The Afrikaans language has a different word for the fruit that Indries ordered (dadels) and the measure of time point dates (datums). The term Coolie is the derogatory name Warders used for Indians, like "Boesman" or "Hotnot" for 'coloureds' and 'Kaffir' for blacks.

During one of our evening chats Zambotla, over my incessant queries, eventually told me what his sentence was. He told me that he was expecting to be hanged since some of the others in his case were already sentenced to death. I was horrified but the calm manner in which he spoke about his fate and the fact that he was always there with help and advice had a profound effect on me. It seemed to have jolted me out of my preoccupation with my own woes. Later that month the 'Prison Crier' (a term I already used as analogous to the Town Crier of old (or the 'Malboet" in the Afrikaans terminology of the Bo-Kaap) who brought the news to the people, came to call Zambotla. He left and we never saw him again. That night I could not sleep. It took some time to gain some measure of control over my mind. Even today I still think of him with a prayer and with gratitude in my heart for the support he gave me during my early prison days. We had a cell memorial service when confirmation of his excecution arrived through the news systems   In 2005 I was happy to learn that his body was exhumed and reburied in a free area outside prison and with a proper service.

Immediately we got into the cells after a day of hard labour we would rush to wash off the sweat and dust from the quarry and get on with our studies and classes. The washing too I had to get used to. There were three showers in the bathroom of each cell but sea water was piped through it and we preferred to use water from the 'drinking water tap' despite the threat of being put on charge for wasting drinking water if caught simply because the soap did not lather in the sea water and sea water leaves you sticky after the 'bath'. The drinking water tap was in a corner about a metre from the floor and it required various contortions and movements of the body to achieve a good wash down under this tap and, since there was only one tap, we had to stand in a queue. If there was a bucket available then this water was used to fill a washbasin from the drinking tap and that made bathing much easier and faster. Then there was the problem of drying off. The 'towel' we were issued with was a dish cloth about 25cm by 35cm and to achieve maximum drying effect the water droplets first needed to be wiped off the skin with the hands before using the 'towel' otherwise it became soaked before the body was properly dried. Washing in winter was obviously a bit more stressful especially early morning during winter months. During the early days bathing was compulsory every morning under the supervision of warders armed with pickaxe handles. I then again came to understand the origin of criminal terminology "going to bath" (jy gaan bad) as synonymous to "going to jail". The terminology "you went to bath" was also used to mean going to the punishment cells since the bathing regiment was a lot more rigorously enforced there and I remember the periods of shivering for hours in the punishment cells after baths under the cold seawater showers at five o'clock on winter mornings when I later ended up there. Supervised bathing fortunately soon stopped since we made it appear to be fun and also because of the time constraints. 'Work' in the quarry had an inexplicable urgency and we were rushed through the morning chores of breakfast and work parades in order to go to the quarry with minimum time loss. Later kitchen staffs that were locked into their cells after seven o'clock in the evening were able to bring buckets of hot water from the kitchen, which they poured through the window so that it cascaded over the interior sill into the tub under the sill. I remember the sheer luxury of a hot bath after a year of cold water. The hot water was obtained from the excess of the water used to cook the previous lunch in and was thus a bit starchy but this did not matter. The starch was certainly better for the skin than the salt from the seawater showers.

The feature of prison life that struck me most was the extent to which we became so completely familiar with one another. There was nothing personal or private. I must have been the only tutor who explained the principles of Mathematics to students who could not wait to get on with their studies standing naked at the wash basin or whilst sitting on a toilet. Letters from our families were public property and we read one another's letters. I thus knew about Nofirst, wife of Goliath Hloyi or Ncanda's Nolisiti. I became a sipali (brother-in-law) to Simon Brander because I came to know his sister who wrote to him. I also became acquainted with Klaas Mashishi's Martha. Martha wrote very soulful letters. The letters from my good friend Ajam who became Professor of Education at the University of the Western Cape was much sought after. His letters did much to help me remain in contact with the culture of the Bo-Kaap where I grew up and I read with interest about the various characters there that I was about to forget; the colourful people from the Bo-Kaap with their quaint nicknames like Muntjie Aap, Janap Skaap and Salie rottekop.   He reminded me that Salie got the nickname of Rottekop (which meant 'rat head') because his wife used to cut his hair and her lack of expertise resulted in his hair looking like the rats did the trimming with their teeth. He also reminded me once more of the controversy of the origin of the name Dullah Kak (kak meaning shit), one of the other interesting characters of the Bo-Kaap. Was it because of his temper (which was 'shitty') or perhaps because he was left handed. The left hand is the 'kak hand' in the lexicon of the Bo-Kaap.

Study period lasted until seven o'clock. Classes took place during study period with the teachers quietly addressing their respective classes. At first the warders thought that these groupings were political meetings and tried to disperse them by shouting threats through the window. The common law prisoners who were amongst us during those early years used to call the warders saying; "Baas die Poqo's is besig om to politiek" (Master the political prisoners (Poqos) are busy politicking). We, with great patience would point out to the warders and their officers that in terms of the Prison regulations prisoners were encouraged to study and these were classes and our way of helping one another with studies.   This was in fact in contradiction of the policy of the Prison Department that required prisoners to be treated and to regard themselves as individuals with no interaction with one another. This was spelt out by their demand that prisoners must 'look after their own ticket', yet they were the first to break it by collective punishments. Of course warders looking into the cell from outside had no way to determine if the gathering was a political meeting or a class of students. Political education or meetings were, however, reserved for weekends.

After the study period it was news time. News was summarized from the snippets of Cape Argus, Cape Times or the Burger the common law prisoners who worked in 'Town' smuggled in for us. Articles from the Afrikaans newspapers such as "Die Burger" had to be translated. Possession of newspapers and news distribution was the number one prison offence and we had to be very careful. Punishments like "meal stops, spare diets with solitary confinement and even assaults or straight jackets were reserved for anybody found with news. Each cell had an informal news representative whose job was to gather or memorize news obtained from news meetings in the quarry. When Uncle George Naicker was found with a radio 'donated' by a common law prisoner who 'borrowed' it from his work in the Town, he was promptly put into a straight jacket. I was placed in chains when later caught with a radio but perhaps my case was not quite the same since I also had other charges and other unauthorized articles on me then. The irony was that straight jackets were supposed to be used to control the mentally insane and I wondered if the message from the Government or its underlings was that newspaper smugglers or purveyors of news were insane.

Every night before turning round to sleep I spent some time thinking about escape. Escape was a challenge that never left. To me it was a project. I was always examining situations for the possibility of escape. Even today whenever I enter a building I look how to get out if the door closes and locks. Some of my fellow prisoners wanted to join in; others were terrified and begged me not to indulge in such 'dangerous' thoughts or activities. They were also afraid of repercussions that would affect the 'innocent'. I read some of the world war two books from the Prison Library and noted that to escape was obligatory for soldiers captured by the enemy. Refusing to escape could be construed as desertion and I fully agreed with this philosophy.

The struggle was really outside the walls of the prison. I read the book by Bernard Sacks where he said that in a struggle the participants need to stay out of prison (not get caught) for as long as possible and once in prison must prepare themselves to re-enter the struggle as soon as possible.

Another interesting phenomenon of cell life for us was the nature of the rivalry between the two major political organizations, the African National Congress (ANC) and the Pan Africanist Congress (PAC). There was only three other organizations represented on Robben Island during the time and that was The African People's Democratic Union of South Africa (APDUSA) represented by one person, ARM (African Resistant Movement and the NLF. It must be remembered that the PAC broke away from the ANC who they accused of not being revolutionary and militant enough. The PAC outnumbered the ANC by quite a large margin during the sixties and I think this was the main reason why all political prisoners were all called Poqo's, after the then military wing of the PAC. The PAC also did not like the communist leanings of some of the members or a faction of the ANC saying that a foreign ideology should not be imported into Africa. The debate went around the extent to which Russia was really communist or socialist or practicing a form of 'state capitalism' and how the application of communism differed in Russia, China and Cuba. We in Africa, the PAC said, should not be one sided but should instead be "positively neutral" meaning we must take what is good from both the east and the west. There were some who remembered Walter Sisulu's support of Lembede's anti communist leanings in the late forties. Harry Gwala, a then ardent communist, denounced almost everything as 'petty bourgeois' and only a full centrally planned economy for the country would work and speed up the redistribution of wealth and land and thus eliminate poverty. Slogans such as "From each according to his ability and to each according to his needs" were heard and often discussed during those early days. There was much reference to the "haves and the have nots" and the dictatorship of the proletariat. The ANC on the other hand accused the PAC of being chauvinistic as well as racist because they only admitted people who were black as members. The PAC denied this saying that the only requirement for membership was total commitment to Africa and they cited the example of a white person Patrick Duncan who was a full member of the PAC. They further held that there was only one race and that was the human race and that their policy was non racial instead of multiracial like that of the ANC. The PAC almost always pointed out that the ANC's policy of multi racialism actually amounted to "racialism multiplied". The ANC also ridiculed the PAC dream of a united Africa. The idea of some form of unification of Africa was laughed at by the ANC as a "pipe dream" or "pie in the sky". Africa was too diverse, multi cultural and multi linguistic with an even greater diversity of religions, economies and development. The current African leaders like Nkrumah and Nasser, they said, were not 'socialist' enough but the PAC referred to them as African Socialists, which was distinctly African.

During those early days political lectures were delivered cell wide and discussions were interesting and heated but with the threat of becoming more than just heated. Eventually the ANC members withdrew from the discussions and sat passively listening and then some turned their back on the proceedings. One must remember that the ANC had fewer members on Robben Island at that stage and hence their political theorists were also fewer. Indries Naidoo in his book wants us to believe that the ANC soon outnumbered the PAC. A quick count of the soccer clubs and their membership list will disprove this contention very quickly. The tragedy was that when these public exchanges between the organizations became negative and derogatory it inhibited the development of critical political evaluation and thinking; but arguments that might become too emotional were particularly undesirable in a tense environment such as a prison. We should, I realized then, rather look towards activities that would unite us as a community.

The PAC, I thought, was rather well organized to resist the possible effects of prison. Every morning was greeted with the PAC salute of "Izwe Lethu" (Our Land) intones in a loud voice by somebody in the cell followed by a chorus of … iAfrika! (the prescribed response). This was then followed by a brief PAC freedom song and a short rededication to the struggle with words like: "Forward then to independence, to independence now, tomorrow the Giant Monolithic State of Afrika" or "We shall serve, we shall suffer, we shall sacrifice" (the three S's of the PAC symbolism). During these morning sessions the ANC members maintained either a respectful or scornful silence depending on each individual's level of maturity and tolerance for political differences. Some of the PAC freedom songs were specially composed and had immense dignity. The song "Give a thought to Afrika" was for me particularly moving and Moseneke sang this very well with his clear mezzo voice into which a deeper voiced chorus blended in. The songs that the ANC occasionally sang in their group after their Sunday political educational lecture seemed more joyous and exuberant. Every organization's (that is both PAC and ANC) meeting was closed by a freedom song and the organization's salute. Some of the ANC members saluted with the words 'Mayibuye' lifting the thumb, others from a different faction with Amandla, lifting the clenched fist but the clenched fist soon completely replaced the thumb. I was later told that some of the ANC songs were adapted wedding songs and hence the joyous sounds whereas some of the PAC freedom songs (such as 'Give a thought to Africa') were adaptations from devotional music. One of the more stirring songs of the ANC was about the People's flag that is deep and red because it covered their martyred dead - known as the First Nationale, which Harry Gwala led with his deep base voice. Another inspiring ANC song was "When freedom comes along" also sang in a deep base. Unfortunately there were not many more phrases to this song.

Political lectures in the PAC corner dealt with the history and values of Africanism, the early Africanist like Marcus Garvey, and the concept of positive neutrality that claimed a readiness to take concepts, ideas and practices from both the east and the west in an eclectic manner but with grave suspicions of American imperialism with its ruthless CIA. The lectures by Robert Sobukwe, the leader of the PAC, were recalled for the edification of members who were not present when it was originally delivered. This dealt with oppression, black pride and the nature of government. The dream of a united Africa was extensively discussed. The thoughts and practices of Kwame Nkrumah from Ghana, Julius Nerere with his Ujama from Tanzania, and Nasser from Egypt were discussed and idealized.

The ANC lectures dealt with ANC history, the Freedom Charter, oppression, communist theory, nature of government. The Freedom Charter was so much revered that the PAC started calling the ANC alliance as "the Charterists".

Eventually, with time, as we matured we learned to accept our political and ideological differences particularly at the propagandistic level. Outside of our respective political education and practice we shared whatever we had and served on joint cultural, sport and administrative bodies as true comrades of the struggle and not as representatives of Political Organizations. Commemoration of the death of comrades was another event that was held cell wide with a similar service in each of the cells.

Public (i.e. cell wide) lectures eventually became apolitical in nature. I gave a few lectures on science topics. Cultural activities like art exhibitions came later. I subscribed to Spectrum (a school science magazine), the Archimedes, the Scientific American and the National Geography, the Readers Digest and had regular cell wide presentations on scientific issues as reported in these magazines. I had problems getting these journals and I knew that the sensor's office kept them back and I wrote letters to the supplier complaining of non-receipt as if it was their fault.

These journals thus provided the material for a Science Journal Club. The journals were circulated to all the cells with a circulation list as part of the library service I managed.

One day I reviewed an article that discussed the calculation that a meteor might crash into the earth by the year 2500 that could wipe out millions of people or even end civilization, as we know it. Petrus Mohlala came to me the following day to tell me that he was very worried for the people who might be alive in the year 2500. Petrus was one of the most caring people I knew. He was one of those special people there with us in that 'unspecial' place; people who cared for others with a smile, a ready laugh and with a sense of humour that could dispel negative feelings as if by magic. Zambotla, Blom Makaleni, George Moffat, Henry Baartman, Blues Ncanda, Mtembu Mvoto, Malcomess Mgabela Kondoti, Hector Ntshanyana, Bolisi Qengqeleka, Mzwai, Makeshana from Cook House and Simon Brander could also be counted in this group. I still think of them with a wonderful sense of admiration. Meldin Pistoli is also well remembered in the same vein. He was the Plumber and, during the building operation of the prison, laid pipes wherever he liked, never mind the plans. The net result was that he was the only person who knew where the pipes were located. He was an immensely calm person whose favourite expression was "Abena woly" (the rr in worry becoming an l) which he translated into English as "Do not worry" when asked to do so. He would carry a pile of newspapers across the yard and I would plea with him to be careful. His pet answer would then be "Abena woly". When we gathered news together I would again warn him to be more careful and he would just give me his favourite advice. He came to visit me after our release.

Saturday was also clothes washing day and in the morning the prisoner who I previously referred to as the Prison Crier or

Announcer would come along with a bunch of letters and called out the names of recipients. Each name as it was called out was prefixed with "Hey Wena" meaning "Hey you". Kadalie, a common law prisoner who was the town crier during those early days had a stentorian voice. When he was drafted out of Robben Island his job was taken over by Jerry Leo. Initially Jerry did not have much of a voice but with practice he too developed quite a good town crier voice. Kadalie was to my mind the best prison crier.

During that first month I received a letter from my mother in which she assured me that everybody outside was still well and that she was very worried about me. My next letter came more that a year later since I lost privileges as a result of my contributions to the first hunger strikes on Robben Island Prison. These privileges included the writing and receiving of letters every six months as well as the privilege to study. During those early days I was interested in law and spent whatever study time I had reading Private Law, English literature and Language whilst waiting for University of South Africa (UNISA) registration to open the following year.

Music was a subject I learnt during music periods on the Island during the activity period scheduled from seven o'clock every day and week ends after four o'clock. The Activity periods were time set aside for music, choir practice or physical exercises. Moses Dlamini undertook to teach me the guitar but I could not get beyond the first few bars of "Smoke gets in your Eyes". I did learn a bit of music appreciation from Shumi Ntutu and Bra Jukes. Physical exercise and music helped with depression and 'cracking and one would sometimes see a fellow inmate exercising to the limit of endurance and feel better afterwards.

Siva Pillay learnt to play the guitar quite well and in the quiet of the early evening he would softly strum a popular tune that was very relaxing. Somebody had to keep an eye on the warder patrols since if caught he would be charged with making a noise and refusing to sleep.   I was introduced to the Ragas of Indian music and the jazz of the Townships known as Baclanga and also to the music called "Fourth Stream" which was a mixture of classics and jazz.   Weekends were good because of the relief from the quarry even though breakfast was at 07:00, lunch at 11:00 and supper at 14:00. The stress of the quarry would start again on Monday and carried on the whole week until Friday. Some Wednesdays the warders went for shooting practice or "shooting at Kaffir heads" since the targets were large black semicircles on white paper. And this also gave some relief from the quarry.

Fig 3 View of the prison yard 1970

For entertainment during weekends there were musical concerts on Sunday afternoons. Singing groups practiced seriously during the week for their performance at the weekend. A very popular singing group was the Choppers made up of Vivian Swartbooi, Ernest Moseneke, and Mike Mohohlo. Their most popular item was "Lets make it Love" about a girl and a boy who grew up together and fell in love without them knowing it and as the story unfolds the chorus would intermittently invite the couple to "Lets make it Love". I think Mike Moholo and Vivian composed this item themselves. Applause in the form of hand clapping was regarded as a prison offence as it could lead to charges of making a noise. Hand clapping was thus replaced by brushing and acclaims like "Give them a brush" was heard for very good performances. The 'brush' consisted of the audience rubbing their hands together and loud "brushes" were heard after particularly good performances. A favourite hymn that was often sung was "Peace in the Valley. The Common law prisoners sang this more than often and I thought it had its foundation in the yearning for peace in the perpetually tense and hostile environment of prison and that perhaps peace would come on release or even at death.

One of the most ambitious music projects was the production of Handel's Messiah, the other was the Sharpeville massacre put to music. This reminded me a bit of Tchaikovsky's 1812. The cadence of guns firing was built into the music. Still another good composition was 'Inyikima' (the earthquake) which was composed in 1969 to commemorate the earthquake that occurred in the Cape during that year. I do not remember who composed this but I do know Shumi Ntutu and Bolisi Qengeleka were very much involved with it. I learnt a lot about music from Shumi at the University of Robben Island (URI); how repetition in music could be used to create suspense and expectancy. Shumi used Beethoven's fifth symphony and Miles Davids to illustrate this. The resolution of that repetition would give the music a sense of drama. I also heard about 'tonal poetry'.

Later plays were written and produced. Some of the plays were of a political nature such as the Trial of Ian Smith the Rhodesian Prime Minister who was responsible for the Rhodesian Unilateral Declaration of Independence and who defended the Bush war in the now Zimbabwe. I took the part of Ian Smith.

Another popular cell pastime was story telling especially if the narrative covered the teller's past life. The best storyteller would get the title "Msiki". Letsoko as well as George Moffat from Pretoria were an excellent storyteller but the colourful Afrikaans stories from Peter Stokes, a common law prisoner were hard to surpass. His Afrikaans idiom with a liberal mixture of English was unique: "So kom kry jy bump hy af die straat djy wiete" and I thought his loan word "bump" aptly described the half walk, half hop District Six gangsters used when moving from place to place. I too had to relate some of my own experiences and the story about a white girl petrol attendant in Bellville caused great amusement. The teenager was not really a petrol attendant but must have been the daughter of the manager playing around with the pump when we arrived at the petrol station. Marnie could not resist demanding the windscreen be cleaned and the girl, not knowing what to do complied. When she finished Marnie took out a cent and ordered one cent of petrol just when the manager (her father I thought) came out and heard it all. We had to start up the car and get out as quickly as possible to avoid being assaulted because he went around looking for his baton or gun. I also narrated my experience with girls, university life and bomb testing experiments. Descriptions of District Six were also well appreciated. After years together and memories fading we ran out of stories. Often we would retell stories not knowing if it had already been narrated. Often nobody reminded the storyteller that it has been heard before and some of the stories were worth listening to again.

Warders were the main adverse environmental element we had to contend with. The others were the weather and sickness and bouts of depressions, but one year in the seventies fleas came into our lives. We did not know where they came from. Our bedding (blankets and mat) became infested with fleas and sleeping became very difficult. Some suspected that our enemies, the prison authorities brought them in since they refused to have the place sprayed with insecticide. Ballpoint refills at that time came in glass tubes and we would fill these tubes with fleas to take as evidence to the doctor and the complaints officer on Saturdays. I remember Benny Ntoele, Tony Suze, George Moffat and myself sitting and observing a flea infested blanket and both George and Benny swore that they saw the blanket move – movement, they said, caused by the many fleas in the blanket. I thought it was just the moving dot on a white wall phenomenon described in psychology text books The cells were eventually sprayed but this had to be repeated to kill the newly hatched fleas.

A later feature of cell life after soccer started was the so called "camps" but this will be described in the chapter on sport and recreation.

Chapter 7

Prison Protest

What irked us most during those early years was that the treatment we received at the hands of the prison officials did not conform to the letter of the prison regulations that our lawyer Mr. Dallah Omar gave us before we came to Robben Island. Unfortunately our copy of the Prison Regulations was confiscated and our demand to have it back was continually refused. Assaults were regular. The food had worms or stones in and often the food that was served was watery and inadequate to sustain hard labour and we lost weight. The vegetables that the prison diet provided lacked variety. We were on boiled onions for weeks on end. The morning soup was made into a paste and plunked on top of ice-cold porridge. This was unsatisfactory and should have been separated from the sugar. The cold insipid porridge was difficult to eat. We objected to the porridge twice a day for F-diets and food along racial lines. We asked why the difference and were told that the prison department policy was to provide food at a level just above the standard to which each 'race' was used to in their lives outside prison. It was explained that blacks for example did not wear shoes or eat bread outside hence providing bread would result in a black prisoner living at a higher standard of living than an average black outside prison and so it was for all the elements and resources of living.   This was unacceptable.

To make the food problem worse, the criminals who worked in the kitchen often stole food and smuggled it to their gang bosses. This smuggled food, dressed up as 'prison pies" called 'ndalaf' was also bartered for tobacco and other luxuries.   Sometimes PAC or ANC members succumbed to this practice. Since the PAC were greater in numbers and had a greater number of common law prisoners who became politically conscious, but not as yet socialized, smuggling of food appeared to have been more common amongst the PAC.   Both organizations tried their best to control this practice.   The only instrument of discipline in the hands of the committees set up to maintain internal discipline was to sentence those who transgressed our rules to a period of ostracism.   One of the PAC leaders lost his eye trying to physically control the practice of food smuggling. The prison authorities on the other hand refused to exercise consistent control over this practice and instead exploited it to create division. It was very unfortunate that some of our less thoughtful political prisoners succumbed to this ruse on the part of the warders and accused their sister organizations of supporting this mal practice.   They must have thought that they could enhance their organization's status by finding fault with others. Fortunately this was minimal and we soon learnt to stand together. We wanted some of our own people to cook and look after the food.

The work in the quarry was another source of complaint. It was senseless and the piecework system on the nap line unfair and even illegal. Further, the warders were continuously abusive, Mlambo working in the "Landbou" when accused of been lazy found him self buried up to his neck in the blazing sun. He then made the mistake of complaining that he was getting thirsty and in need for water. One of the Kleynhans brothers came to ask if he really wanted water and then proceeded to urinate on Mlambo's head: "Jy sê jy will mos water hê nou kry jy whiskey" (You said you wanted water now you get whiskey).

Study facilities were another issue. The prison regulations clearly stated that prisoners must be encouraged to study. Often study privileges were withheld for no good reasons. Study privileges were often used as a type of blackmail.

The Health care in prison was unacceptable. Those who felt sick had to form a queue at the gate to the hospital to wait for the medical orderly who came along with a tray of medication from the hospital.   Symptoms were called out: "Headaches", "Stomachs", "Throats" each prisoner with the symptom in turn responded by stepping forward to receive the respective medicine. The medication handed out was totally at the discretion of the Hospital warder.   There was no advice on how the medication was to be used and what it was. Often it was one of the 'Misc' families of medication of a previous age that had rather horrible tastes and used to discourage prisoners from reporting for treatment.   One of the frequently supplied medicines was one called 'Misc Diabolica' with a particularly vile taste and often randomly dished out for any illness. We felt that it was a form of meanness.

At one time Louis Tukani was given a suppository on the doctor's prescription with no advice on how it was to be taken. When he returned the following day he was once more handed this rather large looking 'pill' and he eyed it fearfully and said that he had great difficulty swallowing that 'bomb' and he wanted something smaller. He was chased away and accused of refusing to take his medication.

On Thursday mornings those who felt particularly ill were given an opportunity to stand in the queue for the Doctor, but a prisoner was only allowed to join this queue if he could prove that he was indeed ill. There were only two proofs acceptable to the Hospital

Warders: One was that you accepted whatever medication the Hospital orderly dished out and often this was castor oil or Misc Diaboloca. The second test was a pickaxe handle swung to the head. If you ducked then this was regarded as sufficient proof that you were not sick. The theory behind this diagnostic technique was based on the premise that a truly sick prisoner would not be able to duck or run away when beaten.

Lameck Kula who was a member of my 'family group' had a continuous headache that he described as a slight headache. This headache progressively became worse and a dull pain in the upper arm and chest started and I tried to persuade him to see the doctor. Lameck had an immense dignity and he said categorically that he was not prepared to debase himself by taking castor oil to prove that he was sick. With a nagging apprehension I saw him getting progressively weaker until one night in cell C4 he had a fit. Tony Suze, one of the other members of my group and I tried our best to comfort him and Tony and Bennie Ntoele went to the window to call the warders. The warders eventually came with their guns but told us that the keys to the cell were kept locked away in a safe and only the Head of the Prison could get to them but that they would phone him. The Head of the Prison eventually arrived in the small hours of the morning and escorted by a small army. We were ordered to stand back. Lameck was dragged out of the cell on his sleeping mat. We thought that Lameck would be taken to the hospital to receive emergency medical attention but towards the morning something made me peep out into the passage and there I saw Lameck lying on the rope mat shivering as if extremely cold. I called Tony to come and look. The shivering eventually stopped, as he must have died. The warders were not prepared to carry Lameck. This was my first close encounter with death. We raised this with the duty officer the following morning and at the complaints that Saturday. We were told that he was dead and that the whole affair was none of our business. I was so taken aback. Over the weeks that followed my sense of anger and impotence grew and at times became unbearable but there was nothing I could do and the pain continued. I still believe that one of the basic human rights is the right to die in comfort surrounded by family and friends and not alone and fellow human beings blatantly denied this. I even then thought of the warders as human even though they were warders and white. It took a long time for me to come to grips with the grief and sense of helplessness, rage and even shame and I still have episodes of depression and feelings of hurt when these scenes intrude into my consciousness.

On Saturday mornings the prison officers on duty for the weekend would come along with their "Klagtes and Versoeke boek" (Complaints and Requests Book). The simpler complaints or requests were noted. When we wanted fundamental complaints which affected everybody entered into the book, the officers often laughed at us and said that here "each person is for himself", "you must look after your own ticket" or "this was not a hotel" or "Outside you were fighting against their government and now we want luxury". We did not agree with the principle of "looking after our own ticket". We were frequently warned not to concern ourselves with other prisoners; yet the prison administration was ever ready to stop food supply to whole cells for "communal offences" such as 'making a noise (read 'talking') after eight o'clock'.

Weekends were particularly dreary. There was breakfast at 07:00, lunch at 11:00 and supper at 14:00. Those who were charged for being lazy (the now famous "lui en traag" charge) in the quarry were marched off to a cell in the zinc section to spend the Sabbath day without food, water and reading matter.

There was therefore an increasing level of tension against our tormentors that was just waiting to explode. The only method of retaliation a prisoner had was to go on a hunger strike. We discussed this at some length but the situation soon carried us beyond discussion when a hunger strike erupted spontaneously. This was to be our first hunger strike. The older people, fearful the possible effect on their health and not as rash as the youth did not want anything to do with hunger strikes. Again there appear to be differences along political lines but this was mainly due to the fact that the PAC members were mostly youngsters and the ANC were older but there were certainly older people from the PAC who were also not eager for hunger strikes. They were against a hunger strike saying that our health may be compromised since the food supply as it was, was already inadequate. There were subsequent evaluations of the hunger strike and the general feeling was that as our first effort it was fairly successful and I was indeed not surprised that twenty years later Babenia, himself an old man then saying that it was a failure. Partial success would have been a better description. During subsequent hunger strikes there were greater degrees of togetherness or solidarity between political prisoners because of our greater progress towards maturity as a community and each successive hunger strike was then better than the previous. Nevertheless all hunger strikes had an element of spontaneity. The yoke of oppression was shared and when it reached some threshold all that was needed was some trigger to set it off. Claims as to who masterminded or planned the process come later but this is totally irrelevant. The second hunger strike actually started in the Quarry when an insufficient amount of food was delivered, and the process of re-dishing by scrapping off a quarter portions from each plate to make up more plates, was visible to all. This was the trigger and no planning was needed.

During the hunger strike of 1965 (the first hunger strike) I made the proposal that we try and get news and reasons for the strike published in the outside world for a better effect. After consultation with Arthur McDillon and Achmad Cassiem both from the Cape we offered to find means by which our story and action could be sent to the newspapers. By that time Arthur McDillion, the now ex-warder who smuggled hacksaw blades to us at Pollsmoor had joined us as a sentenced prisoner on Robben

Island. He picked up a three-year sentence for attempting to aid prisoners (i.e. including us) to escape from Pollsmoor Prison. He said that he knew a warder Gous here on Robben Island from his wardering days and he could persuade Mr. Gous to take out the hunger strike report and messages. I, with Stanley. Mogoba and Achmad Cassien wrote a detailed article about prison conditions and our hunger strike for Gous to take to Maantjie Jattiem in Cape Town to take to the newspapers. The first transmission via warder. Gous went well. I subsequently decided that this route might also be a good method to send out evaluations of the security arrangements on Robben Island. This would be very useful in the event of an opportunity for escape presenting itself. I drew a map of the Island that was reconstructed from information I gathered from discussions I had with common law prisoners who worked in different parts of the Island. I was particularly interested in the water supply since if this could be made useless we might all get transferred back to the mainland. Warder Gous must have read the second message and took it to the then security chief of Robben Island a Captain Killian. That Sunday during inspection Captain Killian accused the inmates of cell C1 in general of being a bunch of liars. From the subsequent events it will be seen that this accusation was directed to Stanley Mogoba, Achmad Cassiem and I in particular. Shortly after inspection the prison 'announcer' by the name of Kadalie accompanied by the warders working in the single cells came and called out my name and my immediate friends. My handwriting was recognised. We were transferred into the punishment cells immediately. It was like been arrested. With me came Stanley Mogoba, Marcus Solomons, James Marsh, Marnie Abrahams, Achmad Cassiem, and Arthur McDillon. Each of our names when called were prefixed with the characteristic "hey wena". Those arrested were detained purely they were friends and associated. Marcus, Marnie and James were not involved and shortly thereafter released from the punishment section. And thus began my first period of solitary confinement where in the words of Lt Bosch, one time head of the Prison: "There you will have no one to talk to, only me, myself and my nembers (sic)" meaning members of the Prison Service or warders.   Captain Killian considered my report on our prison conditions as a "bunch of lies".

The later hunger strikes were more successful. The hunger strike of 1971 was better. The authorities tried to isolate the 'leaders' by collecting them in the Zinc Section where they were forced to run a gauntlet of batons.   Anybody fainting was immediately charged with endangering their lives and a magistrate came to add a month to their sentences. In this manner Michael Maimane had a month added to his twenty years sentence.   The endangering their life was ridiculous and so was the month added to a twenty years sentence.   Was not the Prison Department endangering our lives on a daily basis?

Another condition we were often faced with besides health, food and study material was curtailment of sport time when we finally were allowed sport. Sometimes, especially when Bongolo (Lt van der Westhuizen) was in charge the accusation was that the Quarry Span had not worked sufficiently hard or work performance was inadequate and therefore sport was withdrawn that weekend.   We responded by cancelling our fixtures and demanding to see the Commanding Officer. Our contention was that we could not organize sport with such uncertainty. We then asked why the individuals who transgressed were not charged as individuals as required by the prison regulations.

All the action available to us was thus a negative response, one or another type of refusal.

The letter in the Archives at the University of the Western Cape gives the minutes of the meeting between our sport representatives and the Chief Warder Joubert in 1972 to illustrate our problems and how we tried to handle these.   The Commanding Officer would then predictably refuse to have a meeting with us, saying that he was not going to be intimidated by our boycotts. We had to start playing before he would see us.

We agreed if we could get assurance from both the Chief Warder and Lt van der Westhuizen who was the cause of creating instability. When we were so assured we resumed our games.

Chapter 8

Solitary Confinement on Robben Island

I thus landed in the punishment cells for the first time accused of having written up the reasons for our first hunger strike and trying to smuggle the report out to the newspapers and also for indicating weak points in the Island security and where its main water supplies were that could be disabled. This was my first experience of many in the punishment cells of Robben Island locally known as the culukoet (cooler). I must again reiterate that what I will be describing are my personal experiences and probably arose out of the attitude the authorities of the Island developed towards me.

The block that made up the Solitary Confinement Section was made of concrete with an outer layer of blue stone that we in fact built ourselves. The cell itself was two metres by two metres. Each cell had a steel gate with a huge black lock and a wooden outer door to provide the inmate with privacy or perhaps just to shut out the air, light and the vision of a slightly larger outside world. Next to the gate called 'the grill' was a barred window that looked out onto the passage and opposite the door near the ceiling was another barred but smaller window about 40cm high and about 70cm wide. The walls and ceiling were painted a drab grey possibly to minimize visual variation and the floor was polished concrete and you, as the tenant, had to maintain the shine on the floor. I am sure the Cape Town City Council's building regulations would not have passed the cell as fit for human living. The ratio of window area to floor area was far too low. Outside to the right of each cell door was a label. My label had my name and number and a big mysterious 'E' next to it. The very luxurious toilet facilities in the cell consisted simply of a bucket just smaller than the size of a waste paper basket with a lid containing a small amount of grey liquid called 'dip' as disinfectant. The smell of carbolic acid still reminds me of solitary confinement. Next to the bucket was a flat plastic bottle of water for drinking. We, the Culukoet tenants had no books and the blankets and the sisal sleeping mat were taken out during the day I think just to remind the tenant that this was not an hotel. The hotelier or keeper of the culukoet was a warder Bernard. He had the long narrow face of an ascetic and would have served well in the Inquisitions of a previous age. He also had the same vacant look of a prison warder and his ever-darting eyes missed nothing. I once asked him during my brief exercise why humans build such vile places as the culukoet and he gave me the rather obtuse answer "Jy behoort hieroor gedink het voor jy die kak aan geja het" (You should have thought about this before you chased on the shit on - that is, caused the trouble). I am sure he did not know what I was supposed to have done, his job, it seemed, was just to make our lives in solitary as difficult as possible in the sense of: "Let this place be of even greater dread to evil doers" variety.

The first month of solitary confinement was no problem for me, even without books. I am not a very social or gregarious person and I thought solitary confinement would not bother me. The weather was still warm and the light in the cell tolerable though gloomy. It was in fact a relief from the hard labour in the quarry. Here there was no Delport with his pickaxes, his wheelbarrows with or without wheels and the other quarry implements of torture. Above all, there was no blazing sun to scorch the last drop of energy out of you. Here, I thought I was going to cool off and relax, take things easy ("lê, vrek en vreet" meaning to lie down, sleep and eat to use the terminology of prison). The warders preferred this status to be called "lê en vrek" ("vrek: meaning die and eat as applied to animals). I was now, I thought, officially on 'holiday' and the holiday slogan "happy holiday!" from my university years ironically echoed in my head. The pain that came with solitary confinement and the sense of loneliness and sensory reduction was, however, insidious and took time to have an effect. I was still to discover what I would call 'eventless time' and that despite me not being normally a very person orientated individual, I too am very much a social being and that variety is not the spice but the very essence of life. Later the sound or illusion of people speaking to me in the night had to be suppressed since I knew this might be the first stage of some form of insanity. The smug looking Commanding Officer who came around for inspection that Sunday seemed to have known it. The maximum sentence of solitary confinement according to regulations is twenty one days. The twenty one days soon passed but the solitary confinement continued and was to continue for about ten months.

For me the tedium started after the first month. Perhaps others endured it better or longer. I am more of an 'introvert' and should have survived a longer time but I am also a mentally active person and the lack of mental activity was starting to have an effect. This may have made me more vulnerable. Unlike the detention at the hands of the Security Police, solitary confinement on Robben Island was strictly without talking or reading or sleeping during the day and there was no foreseeable end to the detention since the prison officials all blatantly refused to say how long I was going to be in solitary. " Jy het mos gelieg en kak aan geja en nou kan jy daaroor dink" was the answer (meaning I lied and caused trouble and now you can think about it). Here were no lawyers, no family or friends keeping tabs, no visits. There were no re-assuring sounds of Cape Town, no music from the Cape Town City Hall bells near Caledon Square Police Station, only the drab grey walls, the gloom and the silence, broken by the raucous shouts from warders somewhere down the passage sometimes interspersed with the sounds of assaults. The hum in the ears that made the silence seemed audible is, I tried to analyse this sound and thought, perhaps it is the sound produced by the Brownian movement of the air. Any attempt to talk even to yourself led to withdrawal of food for the day (known as meal stops) as punishment. The Afrikaans language makes a difference between "geraas" and "lawaai" with lawaai been the more intense form with an element of being deliberate and the extreme term "lawaai" was inevitably used as accusation by the warders for even a whisper in the culukoet ("'n lawaai opskop" they called such whispers). The cold was to come later.

The Culukoet tenants were allowed to come out of the cell one at a time in the morning just to avoid tenants seeing a friendlier face of a fellow tenant for a rushed fifteen minutes in the morning to empty the pail of night soil, take a quick wash under the cold sea water shower and get a fresh bottle of water in readiness for the next twenty four hours. At Caledon Square we shouted to one another up and down the passageways and we had inter-cell concerts as well. On Robben Island solitary confinement was like being in a tomb. The warders were mean and walked up and down the passage in their socks hoping to catch tenants trying to talk just for the pleasure of putting the detainee on a charge for talking or making a noise ("lawaai maak"). Absolutely no form of human communication was thus permitted and somehow the warders ceased to be considered human.

Every Saturday morning we, the tenants, were given a roll of toilet paper, a piece of blue soap and a piece of red soap for washing to last for the week. The red soap had no actual use since it did not lather in the seawater showers. The blue soap was for washing our clothing but this too had no use since we were not allowed out to wash clothes.

So there each of us sat on our spot of concrete floor waiting for the day to pass. The night, when it finally came, was then spent with intermittent bouts of sleep interspersed, for me, with vivid dreams of flying high above the darkened streets of Cape Town. By about 2 am, sleep came to an end and waiting for the night also to pass started only to be followed by yet another day of waiting. Struggling to sleep without success made me realize how little control we had over our bodies. I sometimes fell asleep during the day sitting on the concrete floor of the cell but Warder Bernard who was in charge did not like this. Whenever he was on duty and he saw me sleeping he would open the cell with a clatter and rudely shake me awake accusing me of being a coward by trying to dodge or avoid the 'punishment', the pain of solitary confinement, by sleeping it away. He would be particularly vigilant when I was also on no food for the day as extra punishment for some or other infringement of solitary confinement rules. He then made sure that I did not fall asleep to stop me from trying to escape the pain of hunger as well.

Each human being is given x number of days to live and there you sat and waited for your days to pass. This thought could be very disturbing. Although there was a definite sense of waiting, what you were waiting for was not clear, and this was one of the sources of frustration and anger. It sometimes felt as if I was standing in an endless queue with nothing at the other end yet impatient for the queue to move on. By about the second month or so I developed a cramp in my jaw and a tight feeling in my neck that gradually became a source of pain. This, I surmised was the result of tension that had built up in my body as excess energy that accumulated and then wanted to explode out of that cramped environment in rising waves of an undefined sense of agitation that took some effort to subdue. When I started dreaming with eyes wide open I knew that I was starting to hallucinate and I had to do something about this immediately otherwise I would go crazy.

I tried to relieve the tension by lying on the cold concrete floor of the cell and purposely tensed the muscles that were in pain and then I would consciously try to relax each muscle one at time checking to see if it was indeed relaxed even trying to force further relaxation. Later I tried to relax all muscles even those that were not causing problems, starting from the feet and toes to the calves progressively up the body towards the head. Each muscle or muscle set was tensed and relaxed sequentially until the neck and head was reached. I had to suppress the urge to move from one muscle set to another before the lower one was relaxed. Even when a muscle was relaxed I tried to relax it further. I then followed this by jumping up and vigorously doing on the spot running trying to get rid of excess energy. When exhausted I would take deep breaths first inhaling slowly, and then exhaling with force. After this I would then drop down on my back on the floor to repeat the muscle relaxing routine. This seemed to help.

Telling stories from one's previous existence was a favourite pass time in prison. In the Culukoet I tried telling stories to myself, I would then retell the story of the very religious Mr. van Dyk (pronounced Dyke) my primary school principal to myself who, during deep breathing exercises in the morning before the start of school, would tell us all to say "I breathe in the breath of the Almighty (with inhale) and it giveth me life (with exhale). At the end of the van Dyk breathing exercise he would then tell us to say "And I pronounce everything in my world as good". We, as learners, would then mischievously replace 'the Almighty' part with 'vanDykie' for amusement. Mr. van Dyk never noticed the change in wording even when the whole school was or appeared to be saying "I breathe in the breath of vanDykie". Thinking of this then made me smile. Such recollections from my childhood and earlier existence became a source of self-amusement. I recalled many of these events. The second story that I enjoyed relating to myself was that with Boeta Harpie. (In our community Boeta (which means brother) is the title that juniors must attached to the name of their elders if the person is not directly related). Boeta Harpie was a painter who once took me on, then a fourteen year old, as a 'gopher' or "handlanger" to use the official Afrikaans term for my job description. Boeta Harpie was always in a hurry. I had to pass him the paintbrush quickly, go and fetch his cigarettes quickly, move the ladder even more quickly. One day the bulky Boeta Harpie instructed me to bring the ladder quickly. In my haste I positioned the ladder at too steep an angle and with equal haste he clambered up on the ladder and stopped near the top when the ladder started to tilt backwards. I smiled again when I remembered the portly Boeta Harpie's exclamations of 'Hoei'. As the ladder picked up a backward tilting speed the hoei's also increased in frequency seemingly to match the speed. : " Hoei ..... hoei .., hoei, .. hoei, hoei". After the inevitable crash I had to run in order to escape my ears getting boxed and from a safe distance I enquired about my pay for the work done before I was fired and fired I was. Boeta Harpie was a dear soul and still sent my wages for the day. I smiled once more at the memory of this experience. The peculiarity of this was that I, having lived through these events knew the outcome, yet the retelling had a high interest level for me, which, strangely, even remained with each retelling. Somehow I knew that here in the culukoet I had to keep all recollections involving my family or my female friends rigorously out of these stories.

At other times I tried meditation in that culukoet. I did not quite know what meditation was or how it was done. For me then it was clearing the mind and trying to think of nothing at all and keeping it clear for some time by suppressing any thought that crept in. This was not easy at first. At still other times I tried to think of the infiniteness of the universe and the very insignificant position we humans occupy in it. I would then close my eyes allow my mind to drift up pass the moon and pass the sun and then far out into space trying to comprehend the immense vastness of the universe. I was then left with a sense of wonder. Sometimes I would then get a weird sense of oneness with the universe. This eventually became my regular morning routine. During the afternoon I began doing a bit of mathematics by building equations, deriving their properties and then trying to integrate and later differentiate using a pencil stub on toilet paper. In this manner I tried to give order to my days. I recalled one of the Islamic sayings that "Knowledge is an armour against enemies, an ornament amongst friends and your society in solitude". I strove to make knowledge my companion. Late afternoon it was physical activity again. I practiced juggling using my socks as balls. I became quite an adept juggler with two objects. I could not find a third object to practice three-ball juggling.

And so I gave structure to my life; also filling my days in solitary confinement on Robben Island. Sometimes none of these 'strategies' worked and I would then spend the day in a pain I could not understand but I would eventually recover – I just had to. 'Cracking' in the culukoet would be worse than in open sections and thus a luxury to avoid.

On other occasions I would pace up and down the confined space or jump up, grab the bars at the windows and pulled myself up to peer through the window situated near the concrete ceiling. I would then look out, appreciate and 'drink in' the greater world outside the solitary confinement cell and then drop back when my muscles could not hold my weight any longer. This greater world simply consisted of the boundary wall enclosing the culukoet and some weeds growing outside in the exercise yard.

A fly once flew into the cell and I tried keeping it as a pet. That fly visited me and we spent the whole afternoon together but it unfortunately disappeared during the night. Perhaps it did not like the culukoet. That night I dreamt I was that fly and found myself again soaring above the darkened streets of Cape Town, landing and walking up Leeuwen Street where my family lived and stopping to watch my friends standing and chatting on the street corner. These dreams were particularly strange in the sense that there was some element of control as to where I wanted to go in Cape Town. I had the impression that I could drop down and visit my mother if I wanted to but I oddly thought that I might frighten her. These dreams worried me immensely for some time afterwards. I thought I was losing my mind and I wondered if this was the start of some form of schizophrenia or Prison Psychosis. The dreams were so remarkably vivid.

During weekends the prison officer on duty would come around with his "Complaints and Request Book". When he came along after my first week in the culukoet I wanted to know why I was in this section and was again told that "jy het mos kak aangejaag" (chase on shit = caused trouble). After the second week I also complained about the lack of a Bible. He at first just laughed asking what a Poqo and a 'communist' would want with Bibles so I asked him for a book or newspaper instead and this caused even greater mirth immediately followed by anger. I had been demoted, he said from a D group to and E and E groups have no privileges (rolling the r in the word privileges with apparent relish). I told him that the prison regulation I read did not mention E-groups and he angrily asked me if I was trying to be clever ("Probeer jy slim trek") because if so 'sal jy jou gat sien' which I took meant that I would see my arse or perhaps my grave. Mentioning prison regulations always seemed to cause an irritation even with the milder warders.

I eventually got a Bible that I proceeded to read with great relish. I also asked for a Quran. Initially a Quran was denied with the excuse that no one on the Prison Staff could be found to censor it. I then had to content myself with reading every word in that Bible – even the genealogy. Some months later the prison authorities relented and I got a Quran. The Quran I got from my family was in both Arabic and English I also read this through a number of times. When I read it a third time I started to memorize the text as well purely to exercise my mind.

Later George Peake, who then became the culukoet cleaner when the common law prisoner left, managed to smuggle an old Readers Digest to me and I had a real reading feast. I still remember the sheer pleasure, luxuriously stretching my self out on my rope mat in that grey cell and digging into that old Reader's Digest. I even read through every advert as if it was a fascinating short story. I think this exquisite gift came from Comrade Kathy. Dennis Brutus also sent me the Catholic version of the Bible and some of his poems. I memorized these poems as well. Cells were regularly searched and I could not risk keeping 'illicit' reading matter for too long since the sender might also get into trouble. George Peak had to smuggle that Reader's Digest as well as the Catholic Bible back to where it came from.

After about three months in the Cooler I was called to the Security Office at the top of the stairs leading from the Reception and was surprised to see Spyker van Wyk from the South African Security Police sitting behind the desk of Prison Department Captain Killian as if he worked there. His first statement to me was to explain the shit I was chasing on ('kak wat jy aanja') and other trouble I caused. They were busy formulating a second charge against me for conspiracy to commit sabotage right in the 'blerry' jail and that I could now forget of ever getting out of Robben Island. "Jy gaan hier vrek" (You are going to perish here) he promised. I wrote up a description of how to disable the water supply of the Island by contaminating it and smuggled this out together with the write-up about prison conditions. This then, it seemed, was the 'conspiracy' to commit sabotage'. I then had the idea that the water supply on the Island was a weak link in security. A disabled water supply would, I reasoned, force the Prison Department to close the Island. I had absolutely no doubt that they would find it very easy to 'prove' conspiracy. In a South African Court of that period, anybody charged with offences against the state was presumed guilty. The onus was for the person under such a charge to prove he was innocent. Van Wyk nevertheless wanted to know who else was involved in the 'conspiracy'. I denied any conspiracy but he just laughed and said that we would see about this in court since they had already arrested the other conspirators in Cape Town. They were all detained under Section 29 of the internal security act. He also said something about an official secrets act as the second charge. It seemed that the water supply system and roads on the Island was the secret.

Mr. Dullah Omar, our lawyer, came over and he thought that the additional sentence would be at least ten more years, which would bring my total sentence to twenty-two years. I would almost double my age by the time I was released. I did not mind any additional sentences since we were still naively optimistic that the revolution would not take too long but I was worried about others outside who might be involved. Strangely the outing to Killian's office was a bit of relief. That was the last I saw of Spyker van Wyk until thirteen years later when on my release he served me a Prohibition or Banning Order under the Security Law.

Part of the treatment in solitary confinement was constant movement from cell to cell – ostensibly to separate prisoners who might communicate (which is strictly prohibited) but really, I think, to sustain the sense of uncertainty and disorientation.

One day I found Achmad Cassiem, fellow detainee, co-accused and 'co-conspirator' as the occupier of the cell next to me. During the first opportunity he could get he whispered to me from his cell that I must look under the toilet in the bathroom for a message. The following morning during my turn in the bathroom I retrieved his message and came back to my cell to read it. The message was on a leaf of toilet paper written in pencil. It simply stated that he wanted to study Mathematics by 'correspondence'. That was how I came to write my 'textbook' of Mathematics one page at a time on toilet paper. He reciprocated by sending verses he wrote to me and about me. I could only remember part of one. It was about my supposed girl friend who was

> *"Broad in the beam for all to see,*
> *"She sports a man with a B.Sc".*

Achmad also wrote poems about prison. I only remember the refrain of one of his poems: "Bars, bars, bars, keys, keys, keys" which aptly described our then physical world. The other poem or rather limerick I vaguely remembered was about a man from Wheeling who had a delicate feeling because when he read on the door not to spit on the floor, he jumped up and spat on the ceiling.

We also started playing chess. The red and blue soap that could not lather in the seawater found a use. We made crude chess pieces from the soap. During a chess match we would whisper the moves to one another and each player would replicate both his and his opponent's moves on his chessboard.

With the Mathematics, the poetry and chess the days now became more interesting. I wrote to Achmad about equations, functions, the Geometry of two and three-dimensional space and how it fitted and misfit the world in which we live. This went very well until we were caught. I do not remember how that happened, perhaps we became careless. We were searched and my toilet paper Mathematics book in the form of a thick wad was found in his cell. The security chief first thought that the Mathematics was a secret code and must have spent many hours trying to decipher it. As punishment our food was stopped for the day and we had our 'toilet paper privileges" (that is toilet paper supply) withdrawn as well. We objected and were thereafter allowed only a ration of one sheet of toilet paper per day as a concession.

Warder Bernard took it upon himself to inspect our toilet bucket to ensure we did not again misuse our toilet privileges. This resulted in great discomfort and to relieve this we had to take more of the quick salt-water shower baths in the mornings before exercise in the yard. My little stump of pencil was also found and confiscated. I had treasured that little pencil and its loss was a tragedy. Fortunately George Peake managed to get me another little pencil. We were warned that if caught again we would have only 'rice' water for food for a whole month. Teaser, the common law prisoner, who was the cleaner then and who seemed to be second in command of the culukoet, mocked us by predicting that we would eventually become as thin as Ghandi. After repeated complaints we eventually got our 'toilet paper privileges' reinstated with serious warnings.

Winter finally came to the punishment cells and the walls picked up a damp appearance. The fight against tedium now competed with the cold. The ill-fitting steel window frames leaked in cold arctic air and I tried my best to seal this with strips of folded toilet paper to serve as gaskets. At night I often had to jump up and do vigorous bouts of running on the spot to heat up and bring circulation back since the flimsy little blanket was inadequate. The compulsory seawater baths at five o'clock in the morning became another problem. I then recalled why the prison term for getting arrested (thrown into the culukoet) is 'to bath'. The common law prisoner's terminology for "You will get caught' translated into "Jy gaan bad". Fortunately this bathing was stopped purely because the warders ran out of time since, after persistent complaints, our exercise time was extended to twenty minutes a day and there was thus not enough time for the morning baths and exercise one at a time for all of us.

In the mornings after cleaning our night soil (the little waste paper size drum with some sheep dip as disinfectant) each detainee was now allowed to walk around the prescribed circular path on the gravel in the yard for twenty minutes. There were four of us and we were later joined by a common law prisoner.

Since prisoners under punishment were allowed out only one person at a time the whole process of watering, washing and exercising us took almost three hours. To ensure that we did not see any human face each one of us was marched in before the next prisoner under solitary confinement was escorted out.

As indicated, one of the tricks of the prison authorities was that we were never kept in the same cell for too long. Thus one day I was moved and found a new face in the cell opposite me. It was Edward Gallie nick named Ronner after the Afrikaans for "round one". A round person is supposed to be fat but Edward Gallie was very muscular and very tough looking and far from been fat. Perhaps there was a time when Edward Gallie was round and perhaps even lovable. Since he was a common law prisoner he was given the privilege of a cell with a larger window facing the yard that provided more light. I later came to know Ronner as the 'general' or leader of a very violent prison gang fittingly called the Desperadoes who greeted one another with the raised fist signifying a challenge and threat to fight. The tops of the cell windows were not glazed and sometimes when the warders were short staffed it was possible to talk to others across the passage by standing at our cell windows on a rolled up mat. During such an opportunity I managed to ask Ronner what brought him here to the punishment section. He explained to me that as the General of the Desperadoes he made a decree to the effect that for two weeks nobody was allowed on a section of the stoep in front of the kitchen where the coffee drum normally stood without his expressed permission. The prisoner who manned the coffee drum had his permission. All the other prisoners also respected this decree except a stupid warder who stepped onto the stoep. When he, Ronner, saw this he went up to him to tell him that the stoep was out of bounds to everybody and politely asked him to please step off. He thus gave the warder more than a fair warning and enough time to comply with his order. The warder did not listen and as a General Ronner was forced to take action. I then asked him what this action was and he explained that because of this disobedience he had to discipline the warder. He went to the coalbunker to find a spade to smash the warder's face in. He could not, however, find a spade at that moment and since the matter was urgent he had to use his fist. Of course the other warders intervened and he was assaulted and dragged down here charged for assaulting a warder, found guilty and sentenced to twenty-one days in the culukoet. Ronner had a tally for twenty-one days scratched on the wall and he was counting the days down from twenty-one whereas I was counting up. I asked him if he really struck the warder and he said he gave the warder a pleasing shot with the fist in his 'blerrie' nose.

During the next few weeks I came to know Ronner much better. He also seemed to sit in his cell waiting for his twenty-one days to come to an end. Even though he was a hardened inmate with more prison experience than I he too developed the depression which solitary confinement brings about. I know this because from time to time Ronner for no discernable reason would just call out the words "Hard times Pellie" (the diminutive for pal) or "seven o'clock outie". Seven o'clock seems to be a magic hour in prison and I have heard this often rom various common law prisoners. During a quiet moment he confided to me that he thought of a fitting name for our place of accommodation. He said that he dubbed this the "Stony Place of Sadness" dragging the s sounds longer for emphasis and giving the impression that he had contributed greatly to the nomenclature of places. He also had a new name for the warders here. He dubbed them 'Philistines'. This name interested me greatly and I asked him if he too had been reading the Bible. He disdainfully told me that he did not read Bibles but only used the pages for making Zolls (cigarettes using pipe tobacco). I asked him then to explain the term Philistines as applied to the warders and he laconically stated that they were Philistines making the ph sound like an f. (i.e. Fillisteine) because they are "fillise" and he placed an emphasis on the f. The word was Ronner's articulation of the Afrikaans word vuilisse, the plural form of rubbish.

Ronner gradually took a liking to me and we conversed whenever it was possible – normally during lunch times when the 'villisteins' were not lurking in the passageways. He said that he respected my 'book', meaning what I stood for. I then asked him to explain his "book" to me and he said that his book was simple and that it was to assault or kill informers (pimps as he called them). I had already learnt that the salute of the Desperado Gang was the clenched fist raised in a similar manner to the ANC and I took this opportunity to ask Ronner to explain the symbolism of the fist for the Desperadoes. He gave me a puzzled look but still explained that the fist was "om te donner", the Afrikaans for beat up and what tool beside a spade was better for beating up their opponents. Ronner patiently explained to me that in the absence of the spade the fist was the second best since you always carried it around with you. The spade was obviously not a good symbol since the founding fathers of the Desperadoes did not want the gang be mistaken for a farming organization, yet a sickle was included in their badge tattooed on the forearm of its members (the tchupp as they called it). He further explained that besides the sickle there was also a hammer on the tchupp and a hammer was also a good weapon. I asked him how, for interest sake, could I join his Gang and he told me that he would not advise me to join any other gang since I was already a Poqo (the term generally used for any political prisoner on Robben Island). The word Poqo was used to even describe members of the ANC even though it was a PAC term. Interestingly the warders also used this term. If they did not call us "bandiete" they referred to us as Poqos but in the presence of visitors such as the International Red Cross representatives we were 'respectfully' called prisoners. The Namibian prisoners were called 'terrorists' or terries for short. The warders also seemed to have had no idea what Poqo meant. I once overheard one of them telling of his visit to a place near Rivonia. An ANC safe house in Rivonia was unmasked shortly before this and it appeared in all newspapers. The warder naively described Rivonia as the place where the Poqos lived as if

Rivonia as a place for underground political activity was completely acceptable to everybody including the security police.

Ronner became very protective of me. During times when our food was stopped for one or other culukoet infringement he managed to bring in some cooked maize kernels wrapped in a prison towel- probably obtained or pilfered from Mr. Mandela's section across the yard. During one public holiday when there was a shortage of warders and because we were allowed out rather late he could not get any food but he managed to smuggle a half a drum of coffee for each of us. It was a present from the Poqos across the yard (Walter Sisulu and company) he explained. How he got that drum of coffee into my cell I never knew but when I came back from exercise and the bathroom I found this drum of coffee standing in an out of the way corner in my cell. I believe he must have intimidated an inexperienced warder who came along to assist Bernard. That morning we drank only coffee. Around midmorning I heard a tapping sound from Ronner and he waved to me from across the passage. He had an important question to ask me he said. How was it possible, he asked, for him to have drunk half a drum of coffee and, he swears, that he was not passing black urine as yet. Just as a check he wanted to know if my urine was black yet. He has just been to his little toilet bucket and he examined the urine he passed very carefully. Could I please explain this puzzle to him? I gave him a brief whispered account of digestion, kidney function and blood circulation. Whether he understood this I did not know, but it took our future conversations onto a different level.

By that time I was already deeply interested in Psychology since I wanted to monitor my own possible psychological changes under incarceration with the intention of counteracting the effect. I had heard of 'prison psychosis' although I did not know what it was. Here, in the form of Ronner, gang boss and lifer, hardened criminal, in prison for murder and robbery with aggravating circumstances, and now in the punishment cells with me, was somebody who could become my first Psychology 'subject'.

Ronner had been in prison for more than six years already and it was certainly not his first term in prison. I did not know anything about interviewing, fact gathering or whatever skills are taught in Psychology or Sociology courses. Having read a bit of Freud and others I vaguely knew that psychologists are interested in the development of the personality and the origin of psychopathic behaviour. I had a keen and vested interest in factors that had an influence on the development of violent behavioural patterns and delinquency and here, large as life, was a first grade specimen. I, at least, knew that I could not ask him how he became a violent person. I had to be more circumspect as I imagined a psychologist would. At that time the influence of the mother on child development was much discussed and debated in the literature I read. I remembered reading something about the "schizogenic parent" or the "psychopathogenic mother" and how conflicting emotional situations could cause psychopathic personalities. I therefore asked Ronner if he remembered his mother. Yes he did and he remembered loving her. I asked him if he ever had a dislike for her and he promptly answered that he loved, feared and hated her simultaneously. This blatant answer whispered to me across from one prison cell intrigued me greatly and I naively imagined that this was the substance of Abnormal Psychology. I then asked him what made him hate her as well as love her and he said that she made him do things that he did not like or found debasing. Prisoners become very good storytellers and Ronner was certainly good at story telling. This, after all, is the prisoners' major form of entertainment. In graphic Afrikaans he described to me how one of his irksome tasks, imposed on him by his mother, was to take the dirt bin out in the mornings.

Ronner was soon in free recall mode about his earlier life – his life with an elder brother who took great pleasure in bullying him. I did not want to interrupt the flow but I took a chance and asked why taking out a dirt bid in the morning was particularly onerous. The biggest problem with the dirt bin, he said, was that it fell over and then he had to spend the "blerrie" morning cleaning up the lane behind their house. This is what made him angry or "die moer in" as he put it. But he soon solved this problem of the dirt bin in a way he obviously considered very creative. One morning he got up particularly early and took out the bin and then stayed to observe it (or as he puts it "toe kom norch ek mos die bin jy wiette"). Like Grassy who was my first 'mentor' in the passage of B section he waved the small and index finger of his right hand in front of his eyes to illustrate his act of observation (that is the "norch"). He said that he simply wanted to know what exactly made the bin to fall over. This was not too much to ask and bins, he reminded me, do not fall over by themselves. Before long a dog appeared ("So kom kry jy mos steek 'n hond daar uit"). The dog pawed the bin and pushed it over, then rummaged through it and scattered the contents all over the place (i.e. "die blerrie wêreld vol"). Having found the cause of his problem Ronner then prepared himself to solve the matter with finality. He emphasized that something had to be done so that it must never ever recur and he punched the heel of his right fist on the palm his left hand for emphasis. The following morning he was ready armed with carefully selected implements for the job – a few bricks, a can and a piece of thin wire. That morning just as the dog tipped the bin he rushed in with his bricks, bundled the dog into the bin, quickly covered the bin with the lid and placed a few bricks on the lid to secure the situation. He then had time to pack a liberal number of twigs and pieces of dry wood around the bin and to tie down the lid with the piece of wire. He brought his can out and poured a generous amount of petrol on and around the bin and lit it. He then asked me another of his many rhetorical questions: "Het jy al ooit gesien 'n bin dans, pellie en daai bin het lekker gedans". (Have you ever seen a bin dance, friend and that bin really danced). This is what he obviously observed when the petrol flames on and around the bin grew higher and hotter increasing the level of desperation of the dog in the bin. The dog was roasted to death and must have put up a desperate fight inside the bin. Ronner believed that the dog got just what it deserved, I gathered not because it did wrong, but because the poor dog had the impudence to go up against someone like Ronner, future Desperado and gang boss.

I did not have a chance to speak to Ronner for the rest of that week and almost got caught talking in the culukoet. When I waved to Ronner to start a conversation he brought the fingers and thumb of his right hand together and placed in on his forehead and then indicated with his forefinger down the passage. I had acquired sufficient culukoet sign language to heed Ronner's warning that there was a warder lurking in the passage. (The fingers and thumb together on the forehead, I surmised, signified the brass badge the warders wear on their peak caps). The following Sunday afternoon the warders were again short staffed and I had a chance to ask Ronner more about his mother. From his descriptions she seemed to have been a horrible person if not a witch or at least a harpy but this image of the good Mrs. Gallie may have been just plain prejudice on the part of her gang-boss-in-waiting son. She cooked, washed, cleaned and baked for her family of likely social deviants. Ronner was not the only son but, according to the Ronner version, he seemed to have been the one everybody in the family picked on. His father was absent most of the time and at one stage also in jail.   I then asked Ronner if he had ever reached a state of harmony and reconciliation with his mother and he confidently said that he had but only after some effort on his part. I clumsily asked for details. He then made me believe that he achieved this by means of some form of lesson he set up for his mother. He explained that his mother had a cat of which she was very fond. She was, according to Ronner, always talking to that stupid cat. I had a feeling Ronner was perhaps jealous of the cat. One day while she was waiting for her coal fired oven to heat up to bake the bread she was making, she went to the front of the house to attend to something else. I thought Ronner himself lured her away from the kitchen by causing a commotion in the front. Whilst she was in the front part of the house Ronner came into the kitchen, grabbed her cat and shoved it into the hot oven and slammed the door shut. When she came back to put her bread into the oven she found her cat in it, still in a standing position, charred to death. Ronner was intrigued that the cat was still standing and he pulled his shoulders up and splayed his fingers to illustrate what he had seen. The smell persisted for some time. From what he told me the old lady was horrified and was never the same again after that and it took a long time before she fired up her oven again. He was never again harassed to take out dirt bins and sadly, from the glee with which Ronner related this, it seemed he regarded this as an achievement.

After Ronner's twenty one day sentence in the punishment cells expired he was released. He did twenty one days of solitary confinement for acts of high violence. I was doing a year for writing a little note to be smuggled out that very truthfully described prison conditions on Robben Island. This disparity once more brought home to me the difference between a common law prisoner and harmless 'security' prisoners like us. I could not help but feel somewhat cheated by this system even though I expected it. After I was finally released from the punishment cells I saw Ronner swinging the big hammer in the quarry and I knew that he was toning up his killing muscles so as to able to swing a spade at the head of his opponents and enemies with greater effect. Shortly after that he was transferred from Robben Island and I never saw him again. I heard a rumour that a rival gang in a prison somewhere on the mainland killed him.

As winter deepened the cold in the culukoet became worse and the running on the spot to generate heat took longer to take effect but then as Eddy put it "All good things come to an end" and Spring brought some relief. The cold that summer seemed worse than the previous summer. There were times during the second summer in the culukoet when it seemed colder in the cell than outside. I could not find an explanation for this. The Prison folklore was that the culukoet was built on water and therefore perpetually cold. Sometimes a fit of shivering would start for no apparent reason and I again had to jump up and down, run on the spot and do rapid push-ups to get some warmth. This worried me because I feared that I was becoming weaker. I had heard of hypothermia and thought that I was getting this illness. Perhaps summer was late or just cooler that year.

Towards December I was taken to the reception office and handed a charge sheet. This sheet verbosely stated that I "contravened Prison Regulation 99(1)(t) issued in terms of Section 94 of Act No. 8 of 1959 as published in Government Gazette No. 1352 of 1959 as amended by Government Gazette 345 of 1960. In the next paragraph of the charge sheet this was translated as me having "acted contrary to good order and discipline in that the accused wrote unauthorized letters". The charge sheet labelled me as "accused number one". I wanted to know what happened to the sabotage accusation and was told that I was 'blerry' lucky it was dropped but if I continued causing trouble ("met kak aanja") then they would 'fix' me up ("op fieks"). I later learnt that during the same time Harold Strachan, after his release from Pretoria Central Prison, published an account describing the barbaric conditions that prevailed in South African Prisons. Harold Strachan was charged with malicious fabrications and sent back to prison. Had they brought my case to an open court Harold Strachan's story would have been corroborated with possible embarrassment to the Nationalist Government. On the 18 November 1965 we were brought before a Prison Court presided over by 'his honour' Lt Colonel J.D. Kruger to answer the charge. I pleaded guilty and so did Achmad Cassiem, Arthur McDillon and Stanley Mogoba. Warder Johannes Mathinus Gouws nevertheless came to give his evidence describing my letter followed by Captain Hendrik Jacobus Killian, then in charge of Prison Security on Robben Island.

His 'honour' the Lt Colonel declared us guilty of "acting contrary to good order and discipline, besmirching the name of the Prison Department and dragging the name of its officers through the mud". He spoke English and he actually referred to the contents of my letter describing conditions on Robben Island although these letters were never read in that 'court'. This "acting contrary to good order and discipline" presumably arose from me having been one of the inciters ("opstoker") of the hunger strike and my factual write-up of prison conditions during the hunger strike eleven months before was construed as insulting their Prison Department and its officers. I was told that I was lucky not to have been charged with sabotage or under the official secrets act for having sent out a detailed map and description of the Island (in preparation for an escape) and of further sabotage by planning to incapacitate the water supply of the Island. I was pronounced "guilty" and sentenced to be flogged.

Waiting to be scourged added to the anxiety of solitary confinement. The strong man, Van Tonder, alias CutKop, alias Sopapa who was also the lay priest came to see me a week later in the Culukoet to tell me that he had been appointed to administer the flogging and how much he was looking forward to the event. He was going to enjoy it he said and he was busy exercising and practicing every day. His intention, he said, was to flog me until I screamed for mercy but there would be no mercy. It appeared Van Tonder's main reason for 'no mercy' was because he was under the impression that I thought I was clever (or as he put it "trek mos slim"). To make me even more nervous he showed me a form that was filled in when a prisoner dies during or after a flogging. I remembered the code number of that form was P.D.91.

A few days before Christmas when I supposed van Tonder had sufficiently developed his arm muscles I was taken out to the yard in the Zinc Section Hospital yard and made to strip naked. In the middle of the yard stood a very medieval looking contraption. About ten warders in overalls were present, I presumed to assist if I should decide that this was all nonsense and that I was not going to take part in any of the proceedings planned for that day. I was then told to step onto this contraption which was a heavy triangular wooden frame about two meters high looking a bit like a very large painter's easel slanted at about sixty degrees to the horizontal. It had two rather quaint looking wooden steps shaped like the soles of shoes on the first rung and spaced wide apart and I wondered briefly at the artistry the maker tried to put into this. About hip height was a canvass cushion and I was curious about the designer of this contraption's concern for the comfort of the victim. A bucket of brown fluid smelling strongly of Iodine and a role of cotton wool stood next to the frame. The feet of this contraption had steel spikes that were embedded into the soil to prevent it from falling over should the victim on it squirm too much. There was something definitely frightening about this device which was called a "merry". Since this took place a few days before Christmas that year I had the odd thought that I was about to be awarded a 'merry Christmas' in quite a different sense. My ankles were first strapped to the steel slots next to the steps and then my wrists strapped wide and high above my head to slots on the uprights. A canvass belt was strapped over my naked waist to "protect" my kidneys. I had the weird feeling that I had stepped back into the previous century. The doctor came to check my heart and pulse and strapped down like that I had the rather odd thought that my heart was the only part of me that could still move and I remember it did move rather faster and somewhat louder than normal. I also remembered the psychology text books that claim that under great stress the human mind focuses on trivialities. Iodine was liberally applied to my skin and then the flogging started.

It was not the searing pain that seemed to come as an explosion that took my breath away and had the greater impact, but rather the thought that fellow human beings were doing this to me in a completely cold blooded manner. The effect was dehumanizing and the anger generated was difficult to control. Van Tonder was after all a priest and therefore considered a man of God. The Security Police with their electric generators, their rubber batons for damaging the internal organs of the abdomen and their brutality were after information. Here the brutality was an end in itself. Time seemed to stand still as the torture went on relentlessly with the whole organism begging to get out of the

F ig 4 Flogging Frame

straps and away from the source of pain. Once more, in the words of Eddy "all good things come to and end" and the flogging stopped and I emerged from the red haze that was engulfing me.

After the flogging raw iodine from the bucket was liberally rubbed into the wounds supposedly to prevent infection and stop the bleeding but I thought it was rather to aggravate the injuries since iodine causes destruction of tissue.   I was then untied. Even though my ankles and wrists were released from the frame I could not get off immediately. I had to wait for the shriek in my nervous system to subside. The immediate ordeal passed without drawing a sound from me. This was, for me, a triumph, small as this may seem and I imagined the out of breath Van Tonder looked a bit disappointed. The large button I had in my mouth to bite on and the loss of breath after the first lash helped with this.

Walking unsteadily back to recover my clothing I remembered briefly hovering on the brink of fainting but with effort I managed to pull myself together and kept my head up. The injuries healed years ago but the psychological effect persists.

This form of punishment is reserved for 'enemies' of the department and as far as I know only a very few of us on Robben Island suffered this indignity. Two of these (Achmad Cassiem and Stanley Mogoba) were with me in the same 'case'.

A few days later I was released from the punishment section and taken back to cell C1 where I had stayed before. My first round of solitary confinement came to an end. I had had eleven months of strictly enforced solitary living, with minimum human contact and sensory stimulation not just single cell accommodation. I could not talk enough during my first week back in the communal cell.   I am by nature not a talkative person but after my release I found I could not stop talking. I remembered stopping during one of my verbal outpourings thinking that this may well be a type of compensation or rebound and I must pull myself together. I later observed this same behaviour from others, even after less than a month in solitary. I once also observed a similar compensation occurring on a physical level. For example, the prison ration chart said that we must be given a few grams of fat in the food per day and there was a time when we had no fat in our diet for months on end. The reason given was that the Prison Department was out of stock. Then one day they issued us, I think just out of plain spite, with a mug of hot fat, two month's ration all at once. Unimaginable as it may seem, we drunk that mug of molten fat with relish.

The other strange thing after release from solitary confinement was that everything appeared small and every time I came back after spending time in the culukoet, the environment always looked small and puckered for some time afterwards. I would then spend some time with a sense of wonder again looking at the world and the objects around me as if I had not seen them before. It normally took about three days to come back to normal. This, I surmised, could be some somato-sensory and visual over compensation after the partial sensory and spatial deprivation of solitary confinement. This phenomenon intrigued me to such an extent that I later started a whole research project on the Island on information transfer between the senses using my fellow prisoners as subjects. This will be referred to again in chapter eight.

After my release from the culukoet it also took some time to re-orientate and gain strength and to again get used to the hard labour in the quarry as well as to heal from the assault. Out of sympathy Qengeleka and my other cellmates then changed my name to Sorsanti to help me get over the bad experiences I had had during that previous year. In African tradition people who had a very bad experience or serious illness changed their names to help get over it and to start afresh. I am still grateful for the care and concern they showed me. I also lost much weight. I remembered my first 'mentor,' the common law prisoner I first worked with more than a year ago. He used to tell me that if I ran foul with the Big Six (the prison authorities) then I would become as thin as Ghandi.

One of the warders from the carpenter's section then working in the quarry heard of my recent ordeal on that Flogging Frame and thus knew that physical activity was at that stage still very painful.   Even ordinary walking was still difficult. This warder took me away from the wheelbarrows and stones to help him build the quarry shed that he was commissioned to construct. I held the timber for him to nail, passed the hammer and even did some nailing myself even though this latter activity required some qualification and experience.. The shed was to serve as our dining hall in the quarry. This then was the miracle of how I, a 'scoundrel and good for nothing' in the eyes of the Prison Authorities, briefly became a carpenter in that Stone Quarry on Robben Island. A trade like carpentry was reserved for 'model' prisoners who have achieved the high rank of at least a B-Group and as far as I know I was then still at the very lowest level. I am not sure if I was then still below a D as I was once told.

Warder Lambrecht was a tradesman and perhaps not a real warder and I remember him sitting high on the roof of the shed we were building nailing a rafter and then bursting into song with so much joy, totally at odds with the environment in the quarry. Lambrecht talked to me about rugby, the technique of scrumming and the latest pop music and his hopes for his future. I enjoyed that week working with Lampies as he was affectionately known and I still appreciate his gesture to me.

 Unfortunately Delport came and objected saying that a good for nothing 'Poqo' like me could not be trusted. I wondered if he was worried that something might happen to his beloved Quarry. He further called me a "pure gemors" (pure rubbish) and my carpentry days came to an abrupt end. Delport also again duly reminded me that I was an "opstoker" (inciter) and terrorist saboteur and did not come to the Quarry for a "blerrie" holiday and that I had better "fok" off to the wheelbarrows. Lampies also left and never returned. I think he was transferred or perhaps he resigned.

That evening a wind came and blew the shed down. It was only partially constructed consisting then only of three walls and a loose roof. Delport regarded this as yet further proof that I was indeed good for nothing. Completion of the roof structure would have stabilized the walls. Delport, supported by a group of common law prisoners, later rebuilt that shed himself stabilized with many beams even across the interior space. Nevertheless, it was a relief for me to be out of the culukoet with its smells and atmosphere of deep gloom – that 'Stony Place of Sadness' as Ronner, my gangster friend dubbed it. I remember then briefly enjoying again the sweet free air of the hard labour quarry with its stones and dust as I painfully trudged along with my wheelbarrow of stones and gazed with delight, whenever I could, at the wild flowers growing just outside the quarry fence and at the beautiful summer sea playing with itself just beyond the dyke where the nap liners sat urgently breaking stones.

Paradoxically I felt as if I had now lived through a thousand years and something positive had developed in me but I was not sure if this was my personality, my self-knowledge or perhaps my spirit. I have learnt to know myself better and that solitary confinement and uncontrolled anger would not trouble me again and it never did. I think I have learnt the meaning of what the poet Gulbar called "Fragrant Solitude".

.

.

Chapter 9

Getting Educated

Education was one of the mechanisms we used to remain sane and, I thought and hoped, it would protect us from prison psychosis and other forms of psychological degeneration, which I did not know much about then. We somehow felt intuitively that if we resigned ourselves or allowed our comrades to resign themselves to oppression we would find ourselves less able to continue our struggle here on Robben Island and when released. There was a book written by Bernard Sachs in the Library sent by the University Librarian at my request that advised freedom fighters to try and remain out of prison as long as possible and if he or she was unfortunate to be committed to prison then to prepare himself or herself as best as possible while in prison for continuing the struggle once released. It was certainly not the theory of our oppressors when they started their policy of isolating us completely from the political situation prevailing in

South Africa and the rest of the world. By keeping us totally isolated from the rest of the world we would ultimately forget our struggle. The persecution would then provide a type of aversion therapy that would make us shun our ideals of a free South Africa. We asked for newspapers and were laughed at. We were eventually told that we would be provided with 'approved' journals free of charge. For so-called news we were issued with government propaganda publications such as the Inqubela for Xhosa speaking people. This propaganda publication was translated into Sotho, Venda and other African Languages. 'Coloureds' were issued with the 'Alpha' a publication of the House of Representatives (the 'Coloured Chamber in the racially segregated parliament of South Africa under the Nationalist Government)..

When I came back from the culukoet I took up my duties as chairman of the Education committee with more energy. There were then two main streams of education. One was political education that became the responsibility of each organization for their members. The other was general or 'secular' education. As an educator I would have preferred political education to be considered 'secular' so that we could learn from and about each other and cross feed ideas. This approach would have fitted well when integrated with the material received by those who registered for Political Science at the University of South Africa and from the British Correspondence College preparing external students for the B.Sc. ((Econ) of the University of London.

Initially political lectures were given cell wide. We came from different organizations and therefore differences of opinions were expected. The PAC had broken away from the ANC but some from each organization could not tolerate differences. Tolerance for differences was expected from mature politicians but unfortunately the differences resulted in arguments that were considered to verge on the personal and thus cross organizational discussions were stopped. For some the 'agree to differ' principle just could not be achieved. I was then again struck by the religious nature of political 'education', political ideologies and dogma.

Political lectures took place during the weekends. As pointed out earlier, breakfast was at seven, lunch at eleven and supper at two o'clock in the afternoon. There was thus more time at weekends for Educational activities. Eleven to two o'clock was for formal studies and classes and six o'clock to eight o'clock on Saturday and Sunday afternoons were particularly set aside for political education by all the organizations.

I was of the opinion that political education was not adequate. I then had a theory that political education had four streams or hierarchies. At the highest level of Political Education was the study of the mentality of the oppressor as well as the mentality and consciousness of the oppressed. At the next level was the analysis of the problems of the country and the problems brought about by the oppressor and how these problems might be solved and how the indigenous wisdom and social tools like Ubuntu could be used. This had also to do with the "isms" – communism, capitalism, socialism etc. This would include the influence, overt or subvert, that other countries would try to impose on us as a country and should include "corpotocracies" (the influence of national and international corporates). The other stream was the methods that might be used to spread the awareness of oppression amongst the oppressed in order to recruit them to our cause. At the lowest level of political education is the rote learning of slogans and the simplified policy statements of the organization in the form of slogans. These utterances, such as "One settler, one bullet" or "Power to the People", Izwe Lethu" or "To each according to his needs, from each according to his ability" were designed to rally, to maintain the loyalty and boost the morale of the masses with not much thinking needed. From my observations the latter two streams were rather excessively concentrated on at Robben Island. I at first thought that, had political education remained at the supra organizational level on the Island, we would have produced better and more balanced politicians, but now I know better. There was (and perhaps still is) an interesting theory in Political Science at that time, that as the oppressed aspire to freedom they tend to adopt the consciousness of the oppressor and in turn become oppressors or at best lose the desire to fight for their freedom.   This still fascinates me and can perhaps partially explain the rise of dictators from respected Political and Revolutionary organizations around the world. Will this also happen in South Africa? During whimsical moments I would think that the Prison Department be using this theory in practice since it could explain why certain common law prisoners like Dum-Dum in the Quarry behave worse than the warders towards us.   It may also explain why our present politicians have forgotten their oppressed brothers and forsaken their revolutionary consciousness. Achebe (whose books we later acquired) explained this phenomenon in a different manner. He talked about people who have been out in the cold coming into the warmth (those who suffered oppression and are now in power) tending to fear the cold even more at a subconscious level.

Another discussion was representation in government. Somebody propounded the theory that a good representative would be a person who internalized the aspirations and dreams of the people he represents. Can this occur in the election process? There were also endless discussions about other aspects of the election process in the context of the concept of 'philosopher kings', which happened to be a topic for Political Science 1 during those years. There was thus the hypothesis that the simple election process may elect not only incompetent people into government but also selfish and evil individuals. Corruption and greed would have to be controlled since this seemed a serious human frailty. Would the checks and balances of say a constitution counter and control all these? The USSR was cited as a possible model and the United States of America as a democracy was examined with some suggesting that America was actually governed by the rich and hence not a true democracy. It costs millions of dollars to enter the race for president in America. The excesses of America's CIA were also discussed. In fact political personalities in various parts of the world who were not behaving according to some ideals (socialism) were suspected by some of the comrades to be under the control of the CIA who would invariably be responsible for corrupting them.

The land question was another topic intensely discussed and it was again and again noted that seventy-five percent of the population were allocated a small portion of South Africa. To the PAC the land issue was thus fundamental.

General education was across organizations and I saw Education and Educational planning as one of my duties. Many of the younger members who came directly from Educational Institutions found the continuation of studies fairly easy. The older people had to be re-introduced to studying and for others, such as those in our literacy programme, studying was a completely new activity. The sense of wonder these new students found in the written word was for me an intensely rewarding experience. For some, letters were the only means of communication with their families and this was a strong motivation to learn to read and write. I imagined I observed a new sense of awareness evolving and with it a new sense of dignity developed. To observe seventy year old Louis Tukani for example from rural Transkei patiently spelling out his reader and getting acquainted with the written word was interesting and when he picked up my psychology text book he wanted to know what 'psychtology' (carefully pronouncing all the letters of the word) was all about. The English spelling is confusing and difficult to learn. Why, for example, do we sound the 'a' in tomato different from the 'a' in potato and what is the e doing in words such as were, there.

I was also intrigued to observe the extent to which laterality influenced the reading direction of some of the older students learning to read for the first time. Some had to be reminded that reading is from left to right. For our older students this was briefly a problem just as it is, I was told, with some children going through this phase of the same learning process. The reading direction had to be learnt in many cases. All our students got over this laterality problem very soon except one or two students who battled with laterality for some time. For these the word bodyguard for example was sometime read as "guardybody" or King Henry the Navigator became King Navigator the Henry. That was how I, Sedick Isaacs, became Sir Isaac Dick. This name became so generally used that one day somebody asked me to tell the story how I became a sir. The name was continued until it was changed to that of Sorsanti to help me get over the trauma I went through described earlier in this text (chapter eight).

Acquisition of numeracy was another interesting phenomenon to observe in people who were initially illiterate. When I asked Ncanda or Goliath Hloyi (both well into their fifties and both very enthusiastic students) for example to add two and three they could not give an answer outright. When, however, I asked either of them how many cows three cows and two cows together made they would look at me with impatience and would then tell me not to ask silly questions. The answer was obviously five cows. They would then proceed to puzzle out what two added to three could be. In comparison today when I asked my niece's six year old what two plus three is she immediately came back with an answer of five whereas when I asked her what two cows and three cows together was she did not provide me with an immediate answer.

If we were now to evaluate how successful we were with our study programmes I would say we did not succeed as well as we had hoped despite our high flying idealism even though we wiped out illiteracy in the first three years. Many of our students in the literacy class never got beyond moderate level of reading and rudimentary writing and these were the younger students. Perhaps this was sufficient for their purpose.   It is possible that we did not succeed as well as we wanted because of our lack of training and ability in the area of remedial teaching or perhaps we did not spend enough time with our students (we had or perhaps the environment was just too adverse.

The other school subject that gave us problems was History. South African History textbooks of the time were largely based on Nationalist Party Government propaganda. We covered the European voyages of "discovery" in our elementary classes. This problem was alleviated somewhat when Marcus Solomons got hold of the book '*Old Africa rediscovered*' by Basil Davidson simply by requesting it from the State Library to which we were given access.   Davidson attempted to give a more balanced perspective of Africa's past. A number of us later bought the book and it became compulsory reading for everybody.

Makofana, who was one of the most patient people I know, really started the primary school on a more formal basis. Joel Gwabeni joined the faculty when he arrived in 1967. I thought Joe was a gifted teacher judging from the patience, enthusiasm and humour he brought to his classes. I helped with individual tutoring but by 1967 with the arrival of Philip Silwana, Wellington Henge and Houghton Soci, who brought with them huge teaching experience, there were enough teachers for this level. My real responsibility became the secondary school and the university levels.   I concentrated on Physical Science and Mathematics and joined the discussions in Economics, Philosophy etc.

One of the first problems we had was getting enough books for writing to do our exercises in. The slates we purchased helped but we needed more permanent records of text and exercises in preparing for examinations. Only about forty of us who stayed in C1 were officially allowed to buy and have study material and only about a half had sufficient funds to buy extra writing material for distribution. This was not sufficient for the needs of all our students and we considered every Political Prisoner as a student. Fortunately during that period the building group was very actively expanding the prison and there were brown paper cement bags in fair quantity. My own first writing book was made from square brown paper sheets cut out of cement bags and stitched together by the resourceful Bolenti Kondile and Malcomess Kondoti. Those who had money, and were allowed to study, bought pencils that we cut into quarters to share as widely as possible. It was one of these quarter pencils that helped sustain me in my first solitary confinement session. In order to save on writing paper most of us made our writing as small as possible. My handwriting is still rather small even today.

My committee and I drew up timetables for various standards. We had counselling sessions to help our students choose courses and we sat with those who needed advice with the literacy programmes. Our students were only allowed register with Government approved Correspondence Colleges. This was a strict Prison Department requirement. These colleges were possibly checked first and must have received security clearance from the South African Police. Our university students had the option of the University of South Africa (UNISA) or London University. Later London was removed from the list of approved institutions possibly because it had too many communists on its staff.

To counter our enthusiasm the Prison Department and the warders did all they could to make studying difficult. During the night malicious warders would come along to switch off the lights even though the Prison Regulations stated that in an ultra maximum security prison lights were expected to remain on throughout the night. The switch was just outside the cell door and fortunately those with good proprioceptive sense were able to use a broom to switch on the lights again.

Our books were ordered from Juta's Book Shop in Cape Town or Van Schaiks in Pretoria. Lt Naude who was at one stage the officer in charge of studies, blatantly refused to allow us to buy dictionaries because it was not, he said, on the list of prescribed books. It was not a reading book, he would shout at us, because nobody reads dictionaries. Dictionaries would therefore not be allowed. Another stratagem on the part of Naude would be to delay textbook orders for no reason other than to make studying difficult. University of South Africa Students had due dates for assignments that needed to be completed in order to qualify for the examinations but Naude cared less about this. Naude had a very volatile temper. He earned the nickname "Holhomtoe". Holhomtoe is Afrikaans for "run him in" and by this he meant into the punishment cells. Naude thus had that the compulsion to run everybody he could to the culukoet and thus every prisoner tried to avoid him. Naude's other name was Cofimvaba since he was always boasting that he was from Cofimvaba, a village in the Transkei.

We needed money for our study fees and for books and writing material and there were a number of organizations during that time that were prepared to send money, but many of these sources were soon stopped for "security" reasons or branded as communist. Money now had to come direct from our families otherwise it was confiscated. Our families were often too poor to send us money but some were able to get money from the organizations sent to them to redirect to us. Some of us who could not afford to buy the more costly textbooks would buy a hard cover exercise book and would then laboriously copy the whole textbook out by long hand. Seeing those writing using the wash basins in the bath room as desks and wrapped in grey blankets to ward off the cold made me think of the monks before the printing press came into general usage.

I wanted to register for an LLB degree with London University but, because of my role in our first our first hunger strike on Robben Island my study privileges were withdrawn. As narrated earlier my attempts to send out a report of our hunger strike and prison conditions to be published in local and overseas newspapers caused great anger in the police and Prison department and I was accused of misusing study privileges. I landed in the punishment cells for eleven months as an E group prisoner without any privileges. When I came back to the sections, London University was taken off the list of permissible institutions having been declared a communist organization by the South African Government. Besides this, my sense of been victimized by law was re-enforced and my taste for the legal studies had disappeared. I first thought of reading for the B.Sc, (Econ) with London University and started reading British History. When London University was finally declared illegal by the Prison Department I decided to do a BA degree in Psychology and Mathematics with University of South Africa (UNISA) instead.

My interest in Psychology was heightened by my interviews with Ronner, the gang leader, while we were in the in the punishment cells together. I also had a strong need to understand and learn to resist what incarceration might be doing to us and I thought studying Psychology could help. I further needed to know more about Counselling techniques since there were some of us who still suffered the after effects of the treatment received from the Security Police and I wanted to help them. There was also the phenomenon of 'cracking' where prisoners would go into a period of depression and I wanted to help them too.

We had an objective in our education, idealistic as it was. We wanted our students to develop an ability to look critically at the world in their dialogical encounters with others (particularly in the political arena) and we were going to share the tools we had.

Gradually we developed the practice of entering into dialogue with our immediate oppressors the warders of Robben Island Prison. The irony was that we entered into political dialogue with the warders but now avoided such dialogue with our fellow inmates. Perhaps the dialogue we entered into with the warders was very general and neutral with respect to the organizations that existed on the Island. Even Head Warder Delport, the Red

One ('Le Bomwu), the terror of the Quarry, eventually entered into dialogue. This tendency to engage opponents in dialogue remained with me even after release to the chagrin of my wife. When the security police came to visit me I wanted them to sit down and talk.   In our struggle for liberation we promised ourselves not to become oppressors ourselves.

The other interest I had was Health care.   I was by then the Chairman of our First Aid Unit (with the very competent Tim Janties as secretary) and obtained books about health and sport injuries from the University and the State Library services.   I learnt a bit of physiotherapy, sports injuries and healthcare in general.

Formally I taught Mathematics as well as Physical Science as my routine teaching duties.   Mathematics had to be taught in such a manner to generate interest and to get the students intellectually committed and I managed to get this commitment and enthusiasm from my students.   I think I must have been the first teacher who helped solve equations whilst standing under the shower. Mathematics tests had to be practiced against time and since we had no clock, I had to sit and count off the seconds and minutes allowed for the examination until Nelson Nkumane came up with his water clock.   This clock consisted of a can with a cork float attached to a pointer.   The can had a hole allowing the water to drip out and as the water level dropped the pointer moved down against a scale.   After this clock was standardized it worked quite well for time keeping longer than half an hour.   We used this clock for our quarterly examinations and mock finals for our matriculants.   Tony later got hold of a watch, but we had to guard against random cell searches to protect it from been confiscated and the 'owner' charged for having an unauthorised article.

Another of our Education problems was the shortage of study time.   We laboured until five o'clock in the quarry and had our study period from six till seven.   Between seven and eight was free period and also time for those who wanted to practice music or join choir practice. Others used this time for indoor recreational activities such as playing Ludo or chess. At eight the bell rang and we could only study till ten. All those who did not have permission to study had to sleep. We thus only had three hours per day for academic purposes and only one hour for Classes. It was then that we decided to use quarry time for studies but we had to do this without Delport and his warders noticing. Since most prisoners could by then choose whatever work they preferred – nap line, spades, pick axes, rope or wheelbarrows. We decided to try and run classes at these work places. Timetables were drawn up. History Class for that day may, for example, be breaking stones on the Nap line, the Geography Class will be on the wheelbarrow routes etc. This worked quite well but there was a shortage of teachers. This problem was solved by the simple declaration that everybody must come to the class prepared and ready to teach. Drawing lots decided on the teacher for a lesson before work/class began. This proved to be an excellent method for studying. This was the method of study we wanted everybody to follow even if no classes were arranged. I adopted this method for my own studies as well except that I was some times a one-person class. I was then doing third year Mathematics and nobody was really interested in Mathematics so I gave myself the lesson walking with a wheelbarrow. We started using this method for our university students as well. I joined the Quarry classes in Philosophy and learnt about the ideas of Kant, Heidegger etc. In the Economics class I heard and joined the discussion about the concept of demand and supply and their elasticity. I tried to attend as many classes as possible but this was not very easy because I was so conspicuous and Delport wanted me to specialise in wheelbarrows. Our examination results showed the progress we were making.

The Prison Staff must have become aware of our educational successes. Some pretended to be educated as well as us. A warder nicknamed Mambela said that he did a BA degree in

Domestic Science and Hygiene, another one had a BA degree in Carpentry. Others came to talk to us more seriously about their study problems.

One day Freddy Simon, one of our comrades who worked in the Kitchen, brought a warder to me who said that he wanted to study and was looking for guidance and help. Our Administration had no problem with this and I agreed. Warder De Wett who then also worked in the kitchen came to see me at the window of cell C4 where I then stayed. He explained to me that as warders they see a Promotion Board in much the same way prisoners did but the Board had thus far refused to consider him for a promotion. The Board, he said, chose to accept the chief warder's report, which alleged that he was impertinent and ill disciplined. He did, however, admit that he never allowed anybody to, as he put it "op die kop kak" '(shit on his head'). The Board then declared that he would only be considered for promotion if he completed his Senior Certificate Examination. De Wett was not very bright. I knew he would never be able to pass the full Senior School Examination so I told him to go back to the Board and ask the condition to be changed to one Senior Certificate subject only. A few weeks later he came to gleefully inform me that the Board has agreed that he had to pass only one subject as a condition to be considered for promotion but the Board specified the subject he needed to pass. I asked him what that subject was and he told me that it was Domestic Science and Cookery. This made sense because he worked in the Officers' Mess and in the Prison Kitchen and he himself thought that this was all very reasonable. He said that he was now looking forward to attending classes with me covering Domestic Science and Cookery. I told him that I could not cook and that I knew nothing about Domestic Science. De Wett seriously did not believe me. With all those university degrees, he said, I must surely know Domestic Science as well. I then reluctantly agreed to help De Wett by reading his books beforehand.

In theses circumstances then I became a teacher of Domestic Science. I had classes twice a week at the window of cell C4 at seven o'clock with this one student. I learnt a lot about Cookery myself like what makes a cake too stiff or bread to flop, what agents to use for cleaning. Unfortunately our classes were interrupted. I transgressed some prison regulation that landed me in the culukoet and when I came out the usual kilograms lighter I did not see de Wett for some time. When he learnt that I was back he came to look for me at our usual window. I asked how his studies were progressing and he told me that he had tried the Domestic Science Examination that year. I asked him what the questions were and he said he did not know. He never bothered to look at the question paper but during the examination he put the question paper aside and proceeded to write down everything I taught him about Domestic Science. I was flabbergasted and asked him if he expected to pass the examination. He said that that was just the funny thing. Even though he may not have answered the questions, he said, surely anybody who read what he wrote down on his answer book must see that he knew Domestic Science. Entering for the examination was like lottery to him. Why he did not pass was a total mystery to him. I never saw de Wett afterwards. He was transferred, as any warder was, when their authorities discover them getting too close to us.

My next warder student was no other than Delport, the terror of the quarry. He in fact first became Tony Suze's student. Tony was very good with his hands and became the best stone dresser in the quarry. Delport was then expected to produce dressed stones for building and so he came to depend on Tony for this. Delport also knew of our success with studies. He had been a head warder now for quite a few years and there was no promotion in store for him. Delport then decided to also try his hand at the Senior School leaving examinations and started talking to Tony about his aspirations. Delport eventually asked me to come and see him in his office. He wanted me to help him with the Senior School Certificate course in Biblical Studies. I explained to Delport that I did not know much about Bible and he too did not believe me. Fortunately I had read the Bible a number of times during my periods in the punishment cells and I knew enough of the Bible to get along with Delport's course. I also helped him with Afrikaans. Tony, however, spent more time with Delport and his studies.

I somehow also got a reputation amongst the warders as a very knowledgeable person and a few would come to me for answers to competitions they found in newspapers with dreams of winning thousands but I also had a 'bad' reputation and this made others reluctant to talk to me.

For my own studies I included Geography in my BA degree curriculum and one year for an assignment I was required to do a minor geomorphology survey of the place I lived. This was the only time that working in the quarry was an advantage. I spent some time secretly surveying the quarry and rocky outcrops and the layers from the surface to the blue stone layer. I had to keep this project a secret since I was previously warned that if I sent out any information about the Island I could face a charge under the official secrets act. The assignment went out via the study office as all study correspondence did but the contents were not noted.

My final B.A examination was a catastrophe. The university regulations required that the third year courses must be sat and passed together. As was required by the Prison Department I had to apply for a day off from the Quarry for each examination. The Commanding Officer of Robben Island, in his wisdom decided that a D group Prisoner like Sedick Isaacs must not be allowed to be absent so often from work in the Quarry. Leave of absence from work in order to write the examinations was given only for two out of the six papers. This letter requesting leave of absence from work in order to write the examinations with the commanding officer's note can be found in the National Archives in Pretoria. No amount of complaining could change this

Fig 5 Refusal of leave to write BA final examinations

decision until the very last moment but by then I had already given up trying. The letter of refusal is given above.

I finally completed my BA degree by writing the supplementary examination. This time I was given the six days off. I thereafter wanted to register for the Honours degree in Psychology with Clinical Psychology as major. By that time I was beginning to seriously practice Counselling Psychology since there were a number of us who still experienced the after effects of the trauma we had suffered at the hands of the security police. Then the bad news came. No postgraduate studies would henceforth be allowed in prison. The reason given was that there were no warders to control this level of study, as if there were warders who could follow any level of study. My application form to the Prison authorities was returned and stamped "not approved/ nie goed gekeur nie" but this was not going to deter me. I met a common law prisoner who worked in the Censors Office and I asked him to post something for me. I knew I was taking a chance but I was prepared to accept whatever the consequences if this failed. I gave him my university application form and he managed to slip it amongst the outgoing post. A few weeks later lecture notes from the University of South Africa arrived. I was called to the office and I thought that here I

was either going back to my old place in the punishment cells or I would be starting my postgraduate degree. When I arrived at the study office Naude (who was then the officer in charge of Studies) was present and I thought that my smuggled application form to the university was uncovered. The warder in charge simply stamped and gave me my study guides and letters without even looking through it.

I then started the fascinating studies in Clinical Psychology, Counselling and Industrial Psychology with Physiology of the nervous system added as second major. A month later I was called again but this time by the Head of the Prison and again I expected the worst and that my letter smuggling activities were uncovered. I was partially relieved to hear that all postgraduate studies must be terminated and I would be given only until the end of that year to complete even though the degree normally took two years by part time study. Permission, he said, would not be renewed since the Prison Department did not have the staff to monitor postgraduate work   I thus had to rush my study programme but I still managed to complete the degree with very pleasing examination results.

Full of optimism I then started preparations for the Masters degree. My thesis topic was to be in the area of Neuro-Psychology. I was preparing to study trans modal transfer of sensory information and in particular the transfer of information from vision to somaesthetic or proprioceptive sense. There was a theory that people with diminished connectivity between these sensory modalities are more susceptible to sea or motion sickness. I already knew a number of fellow prisoners who reported seasickness during their passage to Robben Island who would become my subjects and I had controls lined up as well. I was going to investigate this theory. I made the apparatus for the research from material I found in prison and bought a few large circular protractors from Juta's Bookshop. I thus started my practical work using my fellow prisoners as subjects. Proprioceptive sense was measured asking the subject to place his arm on a surface that could be tilted at various angles to the horizontal. This was done while the subject was looking through a small hole in a box. Inside the box was a circular piece of white cardboard on which a black line was drawn. This cardboard could be rotated through various angles to the horizontal. The subject was asked to sense the angle of his forearm resting on the surface to match the tilt of the line as seen. The experimenter slowly rotated the cardboard inside the box and the subject had to stop the rotation when he sensed that the black line on the cardboard was parallel to his arm resting on the surface. Those who could do this accurately were assumed to have good transfer of information between the sensory modalities.

There were also a number of us with Tuberculosis (TB) and I thought that an alternative research topic could have been physical and psychological factors associated with TB.

I had an interest in Physical Education and obtained books from the State Library on the subject. I read about a factor analytical study on fitness done in Sweden, which proposed that fitness was made up of strength, endurance, flexibility and explosive strength. I subdivided flexibility into "extent flexibility and "dynamic flexibility". The latter is the ability to change the orientation of the body whilst in motion.

I studied the fitness index of my comrades using the Harvard step. According to this theory a person could be regarded physically fit if he could step up and down a step height of 40 cm at the rate of 30 steps per minute. After 120 steps the heart rate should be in the range given in the tables for his age group. This information was also useful when I had to divide the population into clubs for athletics.

I again managed to smuggle my application form for an MSc degree out, but the University refused to consider me for registration. I received a letter from the registrar stating that the university could not accept applications for the Master's degree and other postgraduate degrees from prisoners. It seems they were specifically instructed not to accept any postgraduate applications from Prisoners. Because of this dead end I was compelled to register for another undergraduate degree. I choose a degree in Information Science and Mathematical Statistics with minor courses in Computer Science and I started another adventure in knowledge. I learnt to do computer programming using FORTRAN through the post and this was quite a performance. I had to write code and post this to the University. This was transferred onto punch cards and submitted to the Burroughs Machine at the university computer centre. The raw printouts were sent with diagnostics. I then had to study the diagnostics and correct the code and re-submitted my programme. Statistics and Computing eventually became my career. On my release I took further courses in all these subjects and ultimately became a Specialist Scientist in Medical Informatics and Statistics and then Head of Department of Medical Informatics.

My studies in Information and Library Science had a practical use as well. I was allowed to reorganize the Prison Library using the International Red Cross Society for support otherwise this would never have been allowed. I introduced the Dewey Decimal system of classification to the Prison Library. Surprisingly I was also allowed to write to the University of Cape Town for a donation of books. The University Librarian at the University of Cape Town, who I knew before my arrest, responded by sending an excellent selection of books.

Fig 6 Librarian on Robben Island

When the books came I sat on one side whilst Lt Naude was sorting and 'censoring' the books. A book on anatomy was not allowed. Naude, in very unflattering terms, asked me how people supposed to be educated can send us a book like this. The following book dealing with Capital was deemed suitable. Naude, boasting with his excellent general knowledge, mumbled that Capital is about money and hence the book was approved. The book actually dealt with concepts of Communism that at that time was the terror of South Africa as well as the whole western world. I suspected that the librarian must have put the anatomy book in as a decoy. The Prison Library had its own problems. Some times the library was searched for contraband (unauthorized articles), which then required me to re-arrange the library. The other problem was prisoners keeping books overdue. This occurred when they thought the book was too critical of their organisation's ideology or the opposite.

The other postgraduate student during that time was Jonathan Hermanus who professed to be a priest. He had all the oratory skills of a priest and he was studying for a Masters in Theology with an American university. How he got this right I did not know. I thought that he was merely preparing a thesis for submission when released in the same way I was then preparing a master's thesis. I became his informal advisor (I can not say supervisor). He was studying the conflict between and assimilation of the indigenous religions into Christianity that gave rise to the large number of new sects found in South Africa. I joined him in this fascinating world of religions. We studied a number of denominations and how these adapted to or became incorporated into one or other of the Christian Sects that were found in South Africa. The most interesting sect we came across was the "Castor Oil Dead Church" which used castor oil as a type of inner baptism. Stomach cleansing was a practice some of our more rural members brought to the Island and I could understand the transition from water to castor oil as a form of baptism.

To enrich our studies I tried and got permission to subscribe to a number of Journals. We got the National Geography, the Journal of Abnormal Psychology, Scientific American and the Archimedes. The latter was a Science journal suitable for School level students. We ran a Journal Club and this also proved an excellent method of mental stimulation that I was hoping would counteract the symptoms of Prison psychosis, which included "mental vacuity" and "listlessness."

Another cultural activity was art exhibitions with Marcus Solomons, Solomon Mabuse and myself as judges. We encouraged everybody to produce some form of art. I did not know much about art except that some works looked more 'pleasing' and I used this to judge the exhibitions. Natrival Babenia won one such exhibition. By that time Marcus and I were working as painters with Acacia Hoho as foreman. We had the task of repainting the Prison and Head Warder Smith who was then in charge of the yard was not sure what the difference between painters and artists were and we once got entered in the work span group as artist span. I think Marcus was responsible for this confusion.

Music was another important educational and cultural activity. Nelson Nkumane was a very inventive person. He gave us the water clock and spent many hours constructing a saxophone from a dried piece of seaweed. The construction of the mouthpiece and tuning of the instrument took up most of the time. We had gifted musicians with us in the persons of Shumi Ntutu and Mjuleni (known as Mduke) to help with our education in music. They composed, played and taught. Music was important. The greatest musical achievement, I thought, was the creation and training of the eighty member choir for the production of Handel's Hallelujah Chorus under the guidance of Mjuleni and Bolisi Qengqeleka with technical assistance by Shumi Ntutu. After my release I bought a number of CD's of Handel' Messiah but none of these captured the grandeur of Handel as our prison choir did.

The other choral achievement was the production of the choral piece "Inyikima" (The earthquake).   This was written and arranged by Mjuleni.   The Sharpville massacre was also put to music and the part where the police open fire reminded me a bit in rhythm of Tchaikovsky's 1812 written after the Russian defeat of the French in the year 1812.

Dancing was another cultural activity that helped to keep our sanity.   The traditional African dance known as the 'umxhentso' was very popular and I also tried to learn it.   Ballroom dancing was seriously practiced by a handful of those who had a few months of their sentences left.   The most interesting dance to me was the very energetic tap dancing Fred Astaire style taught by the very talented Mjuleni affectionately known as Om Jukes or "The Duke".   Tragedy struck when Om Jukes fell ill and disappeared from Robben Island.

Education review cannot be complete without mentioning the need some of the more rural young comrades to undergo the ungeniso ceremony as Abakweta.   This is the custom where young men in are circumcised and spent some period in isolation as the rite of passage to manhood.   You cannot be considered a man unless you went through this process.   This was arranged by the rural elders in prison for those who felt the need.

Thus, we lived and shared everything and in the process (which we called 'inclusiveness) became educated in more than one sphere, which kept us sane in the inhospitable place called Robben Island.   I think we got a wonderfully balanced education together by this sharing that we could not have obtained in any other place or time in our lives.

Chapter 10

Sport and recreation

The human need for recreation is innate and must be fairly basic in a hierarchical list of human needs if there is indeed such a hierarchy. Indoor games evolved fairly early during our stay on Robben Island. Ludo and draught boards were drawn using soap on blankets and shells and stones were used as pieces. The Dice were made, first from pieces of soap and later by grinding and rubbing blue stones into squares. Some of these hand made dice were unwittingly loaded or biased and it was interesting to try and determine the bias of the die. The dice were confiscated whenever there were cell searches but we always started again. Mzwai was a good dice maker and the way he played Ludo, his supplication to the dice when tossing it and his exclamations and expressions of joy or disappointments when the die landed was entertaining enough to watch. Chess was also played using cardboard pieces with the relevant pictures of the king, knights, pawns etc drawn on it and this too was confiscated when found. We also played chess in the culukoet with twin chess boards in each cell whispering moves to one another whenever it was safe to do so.

Indres Naidoo's account that sport started when Zola Ngingi stood up in the Prison Hall to ask for nominations to a Recreation Committee and finding no PAC responses is unfortunately a mistake. He also confused the chronology of the event. Sport started long before the Prison Hall in which Zola made his supposed announcement, was built. Even the spelling of Zola's surname in Indres' account is an error. There is no reference to Ngingi or Nqinqi in connection with any sport activity in the Archives whatsoever. I do not think there was ever a person with the name Ngingi on Robben Island. Lack of awareness is also a possibility since Indries was not actually involved in the very early campaigns to start recreation although he played Ludo and later Monopoly with gusto. Those who were at the forefront planned it a little more systematically. It must not, however, be construed that we had a well thought out plan. We just acted 'naturally' in the circumstances in which we found ourselves. I was a little involved but was absent for the whole of 1965 having spent the year in solitary confinement.

The 'strategy' was to use the Prison Department's own documentation. As pointed out earlier the Prison Regulations stated that prisoners who are confined for more than 72 hours in a cell must be allowed out for exercise. The specific term was 'exercise' and not just air. During those times we were locked up for the whole weekend starting Friday evening at six o'clock and with breakfast at seven on Saturday, lunch at 11:00 and supper at 14:00 in the cells. This regime was repeated on Sunday only to be allowed out on Monday mornings to go to work. We continually pointed out that this was in contravention to the Prison Regulations which stated that prisoners in closed confinement must be given time in the open air for exercise. Bennie Ntoele was very active in this strategy. We organized ourselves to have this entered into the complaints book on a regular basis until the authorities finally gave in.   There were, however, also other pressures such as the International Red Cross Society and some opposition members of parliament.

Chief Warder Theron once responded to our exercise request by getting his warders to open up the cells one Saturday afternoon and forced us to run around the yard in a circle with the threat that anybody showing any slack would be charged with being lazy. They said that we asked for exercise. Later a huge roller (the one normally driven by a steam engine) was towed into the yard by a truck and at weekends we had to drag this roller up and down the area just in front of the gate leading to the area where the reception and the hospital were being built. We then realised we made a mistake by asking for exercise during the weekend and tat out of sheer cussedness the prison authorities brought a roller for this 'exercise'. In our subsequent request we were very careful to use the word recreation. Ironically, this area we were so arduously flattening became our first soccer field when the authorities finally gave in to our campaign for sport.

The comrades started playing 'soccer' by making a 'ball' out of rags issued for polishing the floor and kicking it around the cell. The clothing span particularly Mdalosi later stitched this together to make some semblance of a ball. Although I say 'we' I never joined in the ball kicking exercise. I then in fact did not know how to kick a ball and had no inclination to kick anything.

The PAC members were generally younger and as such had a greater need for sport and physical activity and from my observation it was the older ANC members not the PAC who were more reluctant to play soccer putting forward health risks and inadequate diet as the reasons. I am not a sporty person and thus had no need for sport. I, however, realized that sport was important to help resist prison psychosis.

It was thus purely because first the PAC then the ANC started playing soccer that clubs developed along political lines. Club records at the Mayibuye centre will bear this out.   In all subsequent sporting codes, we in the sports administration bodies tried our best to avoid this split of clubs along party lines as well as physical fitness abilities.

Soccer started in a very undramatic manner. The Head of the Prison brought a leather ball and just dumped it into the cell. I think this leather ball was a donation from the International Red Cross Society who came to visit us annually.   Some of us regarded the ball with suspicion. Tony and Pro Malepe started tapping the ball and with it excitement increased. That weekend we had the first soccer match – an inter cell game. We soon made it clear that we would be organizing our own matches. Clubs were formed, an Association was elected, Referees Committee appointed and a First Aid Unit created.   We were going to play organized soccer in the form of Leagues and Knockouts.

The prison authorities tried to prevent us organising our own sports activities.   The following figure is a letter from Stephan Tshwete where the Head of the Prison disbanded our early sport committee.

The formation of the Soccer association as an Association (The Makana Football Association) was not along organizational lines as chronicled by Indries. This can easily be verified by reference to Box 7 and Box 8 in the Mayibuye Centre Archives.   Minutes dated 21 June 1969 recorded the proceedings. Moseneke from the PAC was the chairman (Nominated by C Ndlovu from the ANC and seconded by Meyiwa from the ANC) and Indries the secretary later replaced by Solomon Mabuse from the PAC. Political organizations are mentioned here to illustrate that the formation of the Association was not on party lines. Before that a loose type of association was maintained by Judas Mabukachaba (PAC member) and Indries Naidoo for ANC members.   There are on record minutes where the ANC members tried to establish an association with the Rangers FC and Island Bucks FC as member clubs.

After the establishment of the Makana Football Association in June 1969 the soccer clubs remained fairly static, that is, there was very little movement of players from one club to another but the excitement of the competition sustained us till well into the seventies. Although Makana Football Association rules allowed resignation from one club, admission to a new club was only allowed on the production of a 'Clearance Certificate' from the first club. Competitions thus inevitably became stale. The PAC teams were younger and were much more skilled in soccer and the teams that won each and every league and knock out without fail was the largely PAC teams Manong with Gunners as second. Manong had a very specific non party policy and some ANC members joined Manong and became prominent soccer players. Manong was invariably challenged by Gunners which was the other PAC team and the second strongest team. Gunners was followed in strength by Ditshitshidi yet another largely PAC team. None of the ANC soccer teams Rangers, Hotspurs or Bucks ever won a league or a knockout and I say this with a sense of failure as a sports administrator. The other mixed soccer team was Mphatlalatsane. The Association from time to time organised so called 'picked sides' where temporary sides were made up for 'demonstration' games. It was out of these demonstration matches that the incident known as the Atlantic Raiders affair arose. Almost by accident a strong side was fielded against a weak side. The strong side called themselves the Atlantic Raiders and the weak side became the Blue Rock and by another fluke Blue Rock scored a freak goal against the Atlantic Raiders. Freddy Simon the Atlantic Raider captain objected but the referee indicated that this was not competition but merely a demonstration match. A letter of protest was handed to the MFA and this was also ignored. Atlantic Raiders then threatened the MFA with "duress". The 'duress" finally materialised as a sit in on the field during the next demonstration match.   The players involved in the sit in were then all formally charged with misconduct.   I became the 'defence attorney' and Moseneke the 'prosecutor'.   The case became 'headline news' for quite a few weeks.

We were therefore determined that any other sports code would not be allowed to develop along organizational lines. We tried to neutralize and even to reverse this division in the soccer code by encouraging dissolution of clubs, but not with much success.

Nevertheless soccer provided excitement, and a topic of conversation for the whole week. Ncanda nicknamed Blues, who slept next to me, and thus was my brother, was one of those men with a natural sense of humour which was accentuated by his difficulties with the English language. Ncanda not only murdered the English language, he also massacred Afrikaans. Blues was a Ditshitshidi member and I was a Gunners member and competition between us was keen. Whenever our teams played he, starting the Wednesday before the match, would promise me that "tomorrow you die" or "tomorrow is tomorrow". He would then proceed to outline how Bennie, their striker would confuse Sipho the Gunner's goalkeeper and his prediction was that I would then cry the whole week thereafter. If Gunners should win against Ditshitshidi then I would approach Blues and offer him a handshake with the words "Bamba izandla" and Blues would hide his hand behind his back whenever I came near and would transmute the Afrikaans idiom "Watse' into English with the words "What say bamba 'zandla".

Blues and I both played in the third division known as the Maghaus. When the Gunners trainer asked what position I wish to play, I looked at this soccer business and decided that the goal keeper position looked the easiest and offered to play in this position. I did not succeed too well because of my eyesight so I was placed as a mid fielder. The term Maghau had a derogatory tone when used to refer to us novices. We were taught soccer from scratch and I would then find my science students who were first division players to be my coaches and had to hear about my inability to apply the parallelogram law of force or other laws of motion in order to place the ball accurately in the net with the "correct kick".

Fig 7 A soccer match in the late 1960's

"Training camps" were organised by club coaches on Wednesdays. Trainees exchanged sleeping cells with one another so that members from the same club met in 'Club cells' sometimes referred to as 'the camp'.   This had to be done stealthily so that the warders would not notice the swap during the evening count and security check in the cells.

 Thus after study period on Wednesdays half the cell where the training camp was, was cleared. The ball was cleaned so that no marks could be made on the wall. The light fitting in all cells except the study cell (C1) was secured behind its wired glass fitting and hence not at risk of damage. Training cells were allocated by the Association. A Cell allocation schedule can be found in the Mayebuye Archives.

We, the trainees would then make a queue to take turns at kicking the ball (the so called 'correct kick') under the watchful eye of the trainer who would point where the ball must be kicked to (that is 'placed').   Chalk squares were drawn on the wall and the trainer pointed out the square at which we should aim our ball. I had great difficulty with this since whenever I was instructed to place the ball in the square to the left, my ball would go to the opposite square. I am still convinced that the soccer ball had a mind of its own. I think in soccer I must have been endowed with two left feet. I could hardly kick a ball. There were other incompetent academics like Klaas Mashishi or Zola Nqini who also had difficulties kicking a ball but I think I was the worst. I nevertheless enjoyed the new physical challenge that soccer and later rugby brought. Even Moseneke, despite the tendency of his knees to knock, became a good soccer player. Whenever Tony Suze would wonder what I was good for, I would remind him that I was a good swimmer, something he was unable to do but he was often quick to remark that that was a sport that would never be allowed here but the really amazing thing was that one day it was allowed. We were marched off to the sea and told to get in but the circumstances were unique. There was no water in the shower pipes and the sea was the only place for a wash. An 'army' with automatic weapons was, however, at hand should anybody have had the idea to swim out rather than just 'wash'.

The 'team talks', the planning and friendly threats leading up to the weekend matches, the post mortems or reminiscences of brilliant kicks, saves, tactics, strategies and errors all had the effect of adding life to our otherwise dreary existence.

The need to diversify sport was for me a necessity. I knew that any particular sport code on the Island must not be allowed to grow stale. After two years we knew everybody's personal stories. I found a book on a sport called Volley Ball in the library (see Box 40, Mayibuye Centre Archives). I wanted to get the non-soccer players into some form of physical activity and summarized the rules of Volley Ball for distribution and I promoted a sport I had never heard of before. Volley ball is a non contact sport and competition was regarded as less serious. The tricks of volley ball like spiking and blocking took longer to learn. Volley ball took off and became another topic for discussion.   What I liked about volley ball was the fitness elements it taxed such as explosive strength and dynamic flexibility.

I also tried to bring basket ball to Robben Island.   I never succeeded purely because it looked too much like netball, which was, in the minds of most comrades, classified as a "girls' game". In the minds of others touching and handling the ball was an offence on the all too familiar soccer field.

I also wanted to introduce croquette but gave up since it seemed a bit too passive and seems like an old man's game.   Cricket also failed for much the same reason.   The irony was that during athletics (the Summer Games) the spoon and egg race, the three legged race and even the 'getting dressed' race were accepted as events and provided much fun and the fact that they were 'girl's games' never came to mind.

The introduction of rugby was much more successful since it was obviously a man's game and a fairly large number of our comrades knew it already.   It was championed by May Speelman and Stephen Tshwete.   Steve was from the Eastern Cape where rugby was very popular. We set up three rugby clubs and I became the secretary of the Rugby Board which we called the Island Rugby Board, the IRB.   That IRB also stood for 'International Rugby Board' never crossed our minds.   When we set up the Rugby Clubs we were very careful not to have teams along political party lines.   Since rugby had more contact than soccer we had to revised some of the rules for rugby to make it safer.   A permissible tackle was low and if possible never more than a touch and the player with the ball had to drop the ball as soon as possible.   We never played rugby in the field between the sections and the single cells and I do not know how Indris could have had Mr Mandela and company as spectators to his rugby game.   Rugby was played in the big field when the Zinc Section was demolished and only when the grass grew lush.

Lawn Tennis was another Sporting code which I thought could be introduced to further diversify our sport and I had some difficulties in getting the authorities to approve this sport. Box 38 and 39 in the Archives contains the documents recording the development of Lawn Tennis. A letter written by me asking for permission to start Lawn Tennis and for a supply of cement to construct the first Lawn Tennis Court on Robben Island can be found in this collection. I finally got permission from the Commanding Officer to take a wagon to collect cement from the cement store but was seriously warned only to take the cement from the floor and to leave the bags severely alone. My first problem was that I had never mixed cement in my life and vaguely remembered that it must be mixed with a certain amount of sand but information on just how much sand and how much cement and water to use I had to get from the building experts like Ncanda (alias Blues), Mtembu Mvoto and Bozwana Bozzie). I took Blues and Bozzie along to help push the wagon and scrape and sweep up the cement from the floor. A warder armed with the ubiquitous rifle and a warder equipped with a baton had to accompany us as required by the regulation since the store was outside the prison fence. When we arrived at the store the warders told us to go in and get our cement. They would stand guard at the door. Inside I carefully explained to Blues and Bozzie that we were allowed only take cement from the floor and not to take any bags. This was the purpose of the brooms and the spade we brought along. We looked around the cement store and Blues pointed out that this was not enough to make a floor (his terminology for the tennis court surface). Then took his spade and went about digging holes in the cement bags mumbling "the floor", spilt the cement on the floor and swept it up and we spaded it into our wagon. According to Blues this was in conformity with requirements of the commanding officer. I anxiously tried to restrain Blues but he merrily went around digging holes in the bags.

The warders who waited for us outside the store did not notice the huge amount of cement we came out with but when we reached the yard Head Warder Smith's eyes almost popped out. He demanded that I step into his office immediately and angrily rummaged around his table drawer for pen and paper. He first hunted around for a red pen since he felt that the crime we committed required that level of emphasis. It was obvious that he was not familiar to either pen or paper but he was so angry that he could not wait till tomorrow to try and formulate charges which he could prefer against me Bozzie and Ncanda which seemed to range from stealing cement, malicious damage to state property and even sabotage. Head Warder Smith's illiteracy finally got the upper hand and he gave up struggling with his red pen and paper and marched us off to Lt Fourie the then Head of the Prison. When we arrived at the office the lieutenant seemed in a hurry to get home. The lieutenant could only make out from Smith's tongue tied utterance that our visit to him had something to do with cement. Head Warder Smith was still so angry that he could not talk coherently. It finally became clear that he wanted to charge us for stealing cement from the Building Store. The lieutenant told Smith that we were given permission to obtain cement from the store for a tennis court. I think Smith's anger must have made him even more inarticulate. At the end he could only but march us back to the field to go and mix the cement to start our tennis court with the threat that we were going to see our arse (the now familiar "Jy gaan jou gat sien" threat). We were later charged with damage to the cement bags and sentenced to spend a Sabbath day without food in the cooler.

When we started mixing our cement I tried to persuade Blues to make the cement less strong in order to stretch our meagre supply since I was sure that we would never be allowed near the cement store again. Blues just instructed me to "trooi that cement" (throw in the cement). I continued to plea with Blues to be more economical with the cement. He looked puzzled and asked me in his unique language "What say comical cement, trooi dai cement". Trooi was Blues's quaint mixture of the Afrikaans "gooi" and the English "throw". We eventually got a deck (floor) that could just about be described as a cement tennis court. There were cracks in the surface even before the first tennis match but it was our first tennis court.

Warder Smith asked his more clever fellow-warders to help with the legalities and we were eventually charged for taking cement without permission (which was less serious than damaging state property or stealing cement) but the time in the culukoet was worth it.

Tennis took off and we soon needed another tennis court. With the second tennis court we were issued with cement and that was the reason that the second tennis court was of a much better quality. I never played tennis on the Island but the completion of the court gave me a sense of achievement. Tennis was initially not much of a spectator sport but when we introduced it into our Summer Games it became very exciting to watch. Tony became good at tennis as well but there was a fifty year old comrade who had played tennis before who Tony could never defeat.

One of the earliest administrative practices I learnt as a Sport organizer was to minute all decisions and to report back on all negotiations with the prison officials. I learnt to memorise meetings for the purpose of reporting or writing up minutes later. Like politicians we in the sport administration were merely representatives. I remember once when the International Red Cross donated fifty rand to us towards the end of the Prison Department's financial year and Steven Tshwete and I were called to decide what we wanted to do with the money or forfeit the money since, according to Prison Department Financial practice, money cannot be carried over to the next financial year. We made a hasty decision to buy balls and we came back to the community to report our decision. We were told that we had no mandate to disburse the money and the general assembly of prisoners at a breakfast meeting appointed a commission of enquiry to investigate us for possible fraud and for acting without a mandate and to report back to the Assembly. Blues accused us of 'eating' the money and the other good natured heckling can unfortunately not be repeated here. We were duly interviewed by the commission which happened to be a one man commission in the person of Hector Nsthanyana. The finding of the commission of enquiry was to the effect that we had to make an emergency decision and we were thus exonerated from 'high crimes/ misdemeanours'.

I also realised that the physical part on the field of play and the spectator participation during the match itself was merely part of what sport had to offer. The rest was the meetings, the team talks, the match reviews both formal and informal. This formed part of the local news on which communities thrive. We had excellent 'mouth news reporters' like Baartman, Letsoko, Blues Ncanda who 'reported' the events orally during Breakfast Assembly or in the Quarry describing the action, achievements and errors on the sports field from different perspectives with many embellishments, expressions and variations. They were thus more than 'sport reporters'.

As another variation and source of community news we had art exhibitions, quiz shows and plays. This took place more during the end of the year holiday season.

Athletics was the next sport code I thought we should try and establish. I got Tony Suze and then Indries Naidoo to help. We circulated a list to all the cells inviting interested parties to enter their names. Next we had to get the approval of the Commanding Officer. In August 1970 I wrote a letter requesting such permission and support. The response to my letter was very negative. The reasons given for the rejection of my application for Athletics by the chief warder, loosely translated, were as follows

"1. We do not have the facilities to support athletics

"2. We do not have weights (shotput), discus etc

"3. If we do give them permission then we will have to also give permission to the criminals and they too do not have the necessary facilities

"4. This will cause another committee to be established and will be a further source of irritation (ergenis) to the accounts clerk

"5. Some of the items are too dangerous

"6. The prisoners will, after approval of athletics, apply for additional practice time which we cannot afford

"7. During the month of December many of the staff members will be on leave and the safety and security of the institution will be at risk

"8. If the productivity and behaviour of the prisoners were better then something may be considered (but) they (i.e. the prisoners) do not actually deserve it"

Athletics, when it was finally approved was a source of great fun. I called it the "Summer Games." Besides the more serious events such as the one kilometre medley relay, the shot put, discus and the triple jump, I also introduced the egg and spoon race, the sack race and the three legged race. The problem was that the rules with judgement criteria for each event had to be carefully documented. This I did with great care. I drew the plans for the tracks with starting points correctly off set to balance distance between the lanes round the curves. We drew lines for the athletic lanes with lime obtained from the lime quarry. A team of judges was appointed and an arbitration panel to settle disputes in the field was selected. I organised sand for the jumping pit to be delivered from the building group.

One of the more interesting events introduced was my adaptation of "orienteering" to fit prison conditions.   For this event contestants used an information pack that I drew up which gave a descriptions of the item I had hidden in the field and directions on how to locate it. Distances were measured in steps and directions in degrees relative to North (geographic cardinal points). The orientation to North had to be obtained by looking at the position of the sun relative to the time. The compass needles that Bra Jeff made were not completed on time because the Quarry closed a bit earlier that year. I thought that orienteering would provide practice for those who were going back to the "Bush" to join the armed struggle after release. The Committee (with Steve Tshwete as Chairman) agreed with this.

Because athletics would become more interesting with physical awards, we applied to the Commanding Officer for permission to buy prizes. First prize would be a packet of biscuits, second prize a packet of dried fruit and third prize a packet of sweets. We had great difficulty getting permission to buy prizes. Approval was finally given on condition that a list of events for which prizes were to be given was submitted and audited by the Head of the Prison who at that time was a Lt van der Westhuizen nicknamed "Imbongolo" which is the Xhosa word for donkey. Bongolo insisted I count my list of events with him before he signed approval for the number of prizes we could purchase. When I discovered that Bongolo could not count so well, I was able to order more prizes than events by simply skipping out numbers when we counted events together. Bongolo never noticed the numbers I missed. Money for prizes was obtained from a collection list which we circulated round the cells in the same manner we collected money for soccer uniforms. Prizes with certificates were handed out at the end of the Games but the prizes were collected and evenly distributed to the cells so that we all shared equally in the proceeds.

The certificates were hand written by me since I was practicing calligraphy at the time. I also did engraving on pens using a hot needle. These engraved pens were popular items to give as presents to home bound comrades.

From the seventies the Prison Department agreed that the film hired by the Warder's club could be screened for us as well. The first film we saw was screened during the early evening. It was not so much the film but rather the walk to the Hall under the stars and breathing the fresh evening air that was most memorable. It was a fantastic experience to walk out in the early evening after five years of not seeing the stars. Later films were presented in the afternoons on Saturday during lunch time. The films were, however, censored and some were regarded as 'unsuitable' for 'security' prisoners. A number of films were banned but the best remembered banned film was "The Ten Commandments". I suppose the Israelites rising against Pharaoh were considered instigation (opstokery the Head of the Prison called it). In a similar vein the film "Ben Hur" was also declared as unfit for political prisoners and banned.

The following report illustrates the problems and inconsistencies we had with the prison authorities regarding out door recreation time. It is trans-cribed from a letter from The Rugby Board (IRB) to Makana Football Association dated 15 July 1972

"This, 15th July is now the fifth occasion that sport and recreation has been interfered with and its withdrawal used as a mass punitive measure for the alleged contravention of "prison rules" by individuals."

"The reasons given for the most recent withdrawal is both trivial and unstable. After pronouncing punishment of sport withdrawal against some cells the Lt van der Westhuizen rescinded his decision via Crouse (a warder) and Tanana (a common law prisoner) and then tried to use a recreation ban to threaten and bully the Brickmakers"

"Today, in an interview we had with the duty chief warder and in trying to determine the cause of sport withdrawal, the IRB secretary learnt that the Lt has again changed his mind. The

Napliners (stone crushers) are being sent to work because some prisoners did not get up when the bell rang on Thursday 13 July 1972.

We feel that organised sport played under the present conditions cannot progress as it is not conducive to good morale; besides sport is a minimum right granted under international agreements"

"To try and stem the rising pattern of behaviour of the Lt we are requesting our clubs to discuss the voluntary closure of recreational activities until such time that better conditions can be obtained. In order to obtain a unilateral front we humbly request you to also discuss this at your highest level "
   Signed Sedick Isaacs, secretary

Even our trophies were not safe as indicated by the letter from the MFA to its clubs reporting that the wooden trophy used for League Games made by Mr Mabukachaba was confiscated as unauthorised articles by the warders when they raided the cells. The following letter illustrates this problem.

6.14.73

MPHATLALATSANE FOOTBALL CLUB.
Robben Island.
5th December, 1971.

The Secretary,
Makana Football Assoc,
Robben Island.

re: Mabukachaba Trophy.

Sir,
My club wishes to bring to your attention
the following matter.
On the 30th November when the wardens
raided the cells, they confiscated the
Mabukachaba trophy where it was kept.
However the trophy was duly recovered
and is safe in our possession.
Thanking you,
Yours - in - sports.
A.P. Moloi (Secretary)

Received 5/12/71
1. [signature]
2. [signature]
3. Mokgabudi.
4. [signature]

Fig8 Problems with our Soccer Trophy

Chapter 11

The Master key

As indicated earlier in this narrative the day I found myself in prison I made the resolution to resist imprisonment, to continually endeavour to escape since not to do so would amount to desertion. I also resolved to resist with all my strength the possible adverse effects of imprisonment. Textbooks describes symptoms such as depression, mental vacuity, demotivation and affective flattening as some of the psychological consequences of long-term incarceration and I was not going to have that.

The incident of making a master key to the cells of Robben Island Prison must have been my fifth attempt to escape. My second was when we cut through the bars of Polls Moore Prison.

Before turning to the idea of making a key to get out of the confines of the cells, Japhta Masemola and I considered other means of getting out. We were by then convinced that cutting through the bars was going to be very difficult and even futile.

216

Unlike the Pollsmoor prison bars, each of the Robben Island prison bars consisted of a hollow tube with an inner high-grade steel bar mounted on ball bearings deeply embedded in the concrete window frame. This design made the bars virtually cut proof. Cutting the outer tube might be easy but the inner bar would rotate on its ball bearings making it impossible for the saw to bite into the inner bar. To cut through this bar a jack would be needed to force the outer bar against the inner and thus keep the inner bar clamped for cutting.

We first decided to experiment with a jack with the intention to jack the bars open using sheer jacking force. I spent time calculating the force necessary to bend the bar. Lizo. Tony, Benny and I using a ruler made a survey of the gaps between bars in all the cells in the sections and we found the gap between the wall and the first bar at the second window of Cell C3 to be the biggest. This was then the bar we were going to try and jack open. The gap was in fact big enough to let one's head through. We then discovered the theory that if a head can go through then the whole body can, was not to be true. I tried this myself. Bra Jeff then proceeded to make a screw jack from a huge bolt and nut that he sourced from an old cocopan truck. I lived in C4 at the time but for the experiment I had to smuggle myself over to C3 to help Bra Jeff. The gap was between a bar and the wall and the wall was ideal to rest the foot of the jack against. That evening we then tried our jack but it proved to be too weak. The bar hardly budged. Unfortunately our jacking experiments left a deep mark on the wall. We now had the problem of repairing the mark before it was noticed. Acacia Hoho, who was the painter promised to touch up the mark with crack filler and paint early the following day and we could only pray that the yard warder did not notice the scar on the wall during the morning. We discussed the tenability of the "head gap theory" some time afterwards. One explanation put forward was that perhaps our heads were smaller than normal. A better explanation would be that it was between a wall and a bar. If it was between two bars it might have been possible to slip through. A hydraulic jack might have been able to push the bars aside.

After our jacking experiment Peter Magano came to speak to us on behalf of the cell pointing out that our activities in cell C3 will "endanger the safety" of the other cellmates. I think he was referring to the possibilities of "carry ons".

We now decided to make a master key instead. Because of Peter's complaint and for security we decided on greater secrecy. The only people who knew and assisted us in any way were Tony Suze, Benny Ntoele, Lizo Sithoto.

I made it my business to learn the pattern of the key the warders used to lock and unlock the cells. I noticed that the manufacturer of the lock was British and concluded that the measurements of the key would be in inches rather than centimetres. The height and depth of the keyhole was carefully measured. A thirty-second of an inch to allow for play and movement of the key was deducted from these measurements and the width and height of the key as well as the diameter of the barrel of the key obtained. Bra Jeff was able to grind the basic blank key out of a solid piece of steel from the crosspiece a cocopan rail.   He did this very expertly since the only grinding tools he had in his blacksmith's shop in the Stone quarry were a grinding wheel and a whetstone. The escape plan with the key was simple. We recruited a man who worked in the kitchen to our project. Our man in the kitchen would get the key. He would unlock our cell after closing time since closing time for the kitchen staff was an hour later. We in turn would open the kitchen cell after the kitchen cell was locked. We would then have until five the following morning to get away. We had waiting for us in the quarry a wooden frame that could be quickly assembled into a complete raft using two 44 gallon drums to enhance buoyancy. These forty-four gallon drums were in plentiful supply in the quarry since the fuel used by the air compressor for the hammer drills came in these drums.

This basic or blank key was brought in twice from the hard labour quarry for fitting.   This smuggling of the key into the cell required a level of expertise since each prisoner coming back from the quarry had to strip naked winter or summer, stand in a row to hand his clothes over to a warder to inspect and search.

After the second fitting the key came in with a small supply of fat and a candle.   Late in the night when everybody in the cell was asleep Anthony and I went to the bathroom, lit the fat and held the blank key in the sooty smoke until well blackened.   This blackened key was then carefully inserted into the lock, held steady so as not to smudge the soot, strongly twisted both clockwise and anti-clockwise and then carefully withdrawn.   The first pattern of the key appeared on the blackened blank and was measured using drafting callipers.   The pattern was drawn on paper and the key and pattern taken to Bra Jeff the following day. Bra Jeff then spent about two weeks grinding the first prototype key.   Tony, again expertly hid the key past the search or 'tauza' lines and once again brought the key into the cell from the quarry.

That night we once more put up our 'table' next to the cell door pretending to study. This did not look too strange since prisoners wishing to study late did so behind the door to hide from the warders on patrol.   Late that night when everybody was asleep we inserted the key into the lock.   The key turned once lifting some tumblers and then got stuck.   To unlock the door the key must be turned twice and only a master key could do this.   We now had a day key stuck in the lock.   With some struggle and much sweat we managed to get the key out but the door was in unlock position. The 'key' did not fit too well. We spent that night debating whether to re-insert our ill fitting key to try and re-lock our cell door or to leave it unlocked. We finally decided not to risk inserting the key.   A key stuck in the lock was a greater risk.   When morning came the cell was still unlocked and as the instruction to 'fall in was called out we saw the spectre of a period of starvation on spare diet and solitary confinement in the punishment cells that would inevitably follow discovery.

The day warder came, inserted his key and found the cell not properly locked. Instead of unlocking and opening the steel grill he turned around and went straight to the Head of the Prison who came and inspected the lock. After a brief discussion with the warder in charge of the yard the Head of the Prison left. We were then let out. The relief was great. Later that day we learnt that the night warder was placed on a charge of negligence and demoted to night duty on the watchtower.

The key was now taken to Bra Jeff for further refinement. After about eight days the key came back to the cell for another fitting but with it came, quite incidentally, a non functioning radio which was acquired somewhere with instructions to me that I must try and make it work. This would enable us to get some very badly sought after news from the outside world. It will be recalled that the government policy then was to keep all news strictly from us with the hope that in the absence of news we would become 'rehabilitated'. Anybody with even a snippet of a newspaper was severely punished with solitary confinement and spare diet and even straight jackets. Unfortunately, and not known to us this radio was missed from where it disappeared from in Town and a massive search was initiated by the Head of the Prison and the Chief of Security of the Island to recover this radio. We were totally surprised and unprepared when the warders burst into our cell with shouts of "hande teen die muur en staan still!" (hands against the wall and don't move!).

I wracked my brain trying to think how to hide the radio and the key that now resided in my locker. The warders split up to choose their victims under the watchful eye of the Chief Warder. A warder came to me and demanded I open my locker. In the first part of the search the radio that I had managed to fix was found, placed on the top ledge of the desk and switched on and for the first time ever news was loudly broadcast into our news starved cell; the voice of the newsreader (think it was Hugh Ross) starting the seven o'clock news. This was indeed the strangest sound I had ever heard in that cell in the face of the government policy to block out and supress all forms of news. What made it so unique was that I had the odd thought that I was going to be praised for fixing the radio and that there would be some applause. I was very proud of having managed to fix the radio. The face of the Head of the Prison changed into a vicious snarl and an expression of horror appeared on his face. To him it must have sounded like swearing in church and judging from the glaze in his eyes he must have had great difficulty controlling himself. The radio was then hurriedly switched off as if to stop some ugly profanity coming from it. I was hoping that this would be all but the now over-enthusiastic warder was searching deeper into my locker as if now looking for a television as well. My prayer was not answered that night and the key was brought to light and tested to exclamations of great amazement and much swearing and shouting. I was nevertheless oddly pleased to see the key turn smoothly.

The chief warder who, to my medically untrained eye, appeared to be struggling to recover from a fit, shouted at me to take my blankets and come with him. They did not wait. I was dragged and pushed all the way down to the punishment section and roughly thrown into a damp cell. But that was not enough. In the cell I was held up by the arms by two warders, punched in the face and head by the others, dropped onto the floor and kicked about. Half dazed I felt my clothes pulled off and chains put onto my legs and wrists which the prison rules say must be fitted to any prisoner who attempted an escape and having a key seemed sufficient for this rule to apply. A chained prisoner needed special clothes with buttons and short pants like a skirt to facilitate toilet and bathing requirements. No such clothes were available and I was left naked in the cell. Nobody was prepared to go and look for special clothing.

During the early hours of the night I slowly recovered and wiped the blood from my face. I must have lost body heat because I found myself shivering uncontrollably. The pain from the physical assault gradually subsided only to be replaced by the pain which intense cold brings about. I crawled shivering into the blanket and had great difficulty falling asleep. I knew from previous experience in the culukoet that to fight the cold I had to jump up and do vigorous on the spot running but I was too weak for that and the chains made it even more difficult. I manage to doze off when a terrifying tremor of the cell and bars started. The earthquake of 1969 reached Robben Island. This was one of my most horrifying experiences. The lower levels of mechanisms for survival of the organism took over control of my body and the panic reaction was extremely unpleasant. Not only was I trapped in a small cell, I was also naked, awkwardly chained, injured with possibly a fractured jaw, frozen to the point where shivering stopped. That night I learnt what claustrophobia is really like.

The following day I was moved to another cell. From the adjoining cell I could hear activity as a common law prisoner carefully washed the blood spots from the cell walls and floor. He must have been brought in specifically for that task. I wanted to lay an assault charge but the doctor who came two weeks later said that he "can find no evidence of assault". When a neurologist looked at my skew jaw years later he thought I was suffering from Bell 's palsy. My jaw still occasionally clicks and jams up during meal times.

Later that month I was charged with having in my possession an unauthorized article (the radio) and for attempting to escape and my stay on the Island was formally extended by nine months by a magistrate who was imported for the purpose. The proceedings had little interest value to me.

I have always suppressed these experiences and never spoken of them before since to my great shame I was never able to take up the assault case successfully as was my duty as a political prisoner. I was too dispirited and had some difficulty marshalling my strength to fight the pain of cold in the solitary confinement cell with the added restrictions of the chains. Bra Jeff was removed from us and all the locks in Robben Island Prison changed and a piece of metal welded onto the inside of each lock so that access to the lock from inside the cells was blocked.

A month later I was released from the punishment cells and with Tony's support I eventually got over the shame of having failed to successfully lay a charge against the head of the prison for assault. He helped me to recover and to start planning once more. To help overcome the difficult experiences my name was once more changed as is the practice in rural areas. I now briefly became known as Kitso.

After I recovered I started experimenting with short circuiting the electricity supply to the Prison by unscrewing the light fitting in the bathroom to determine how far a short circuit would cut electricity supply to the prison and what sections would be affected.

In 1999 the Robben Island Museum asked me to remake the key and my neighbour George Mulder an iron smith helped me to shape it taking the place of Jeff Masemola. I used the same process that is the fat lamp to blacken the blank to get the serrations of the key. This key depicted on the cover of this book was the outcome project. I made two keys: one for the Robben Island Museum and the other for myself.

The master key is depicted on the cover.

Chapter 12

Conquering the quarry

I think that we, as a community, started on the road to conquering that quarry when we brought our discussions, our studies and debates and the stories of our past lives to the stone quarry whilst going through the motion of the hard labour.

We started pushing wheelbarrows in pairs and passed the day conversing with one another, discussing issues which concerned us, sharing our past and preparing to share our present lives and to dream of our future. In this way we came to know one another more intimately. I still remember many of these Quarry stories. The one by Bra Matthew Mokwena's of the black guy who always managed to get served at the white counter of a rural shop in the Orange Free State where apartheid was at the extreme because he told the shopkeeper that he was buying for Baas (Master) Matthews. There was some strange logic in this in that as long as he was buying on behalf of a white man then he could be served at the white counter. One day after buying a bottle of cool drink Matthew forgot himself and took a sip of a drink he had just purchased at the white counter. The white shopkeeper saw this and yelled at him not to drink Baas Matthew's cool drink to which Matthew responded by pointing at himself saying that he was Baas Matthews – Matthews Mokwena.   Obviously Matthews had to run for his life. Each one of us had a story or two to tell. Gordon Hendricks had a whole series of such stories but the most hilarious was the one where he was too shy to go to a pyjama party with short pyjamas as was required by the invitation so the other guests caught him and held him down so that his pyjamas could be cut short. I related some of the girl troubles I had and how, I tried to establish whether ghosts exist by sleeping on a grave in Maitland Cemetery in Cape Town for one night. Bolisi who was a keen believer in the netherworld was amazed that none of us got possessed; others thought that must be the cause of me been a bit 'different'. Ncanda thought I must have then undergone the "twasa" that is, taught by the ancestors and the people of the river and that was why I was Insanusi. In the rural areas that is the only way in which the Isanusi (the wise men) gained knowledge. Perhaps somebody should collect these stories and publish then under the heading "Quarry Stories".

Like the peregrinators of old we exchanged and shared knowledge and ideas whilst pushing wheelbarrows up and down the dykes of the quarry. One of the discussions which carried on for some time was the problem of a bullet going at 100 km per hour shot from a train going at the same speed. Would the bullet and the train now move together since both would be going at 100 km per hour?   What if the bullet was shot in the opposite direction to the motion of the train? I at first just listened and later attempted an explanation in terms of vectors. We thus made that quarry a segment of our university. This made the tedium bearable and ironically we even looked forward to the day.

This took then away much of the soul killing monotony of the quarry. I started to learn Xhosa on the wheelbarrow route and became intrigued with the rhythm of this new language.

The classes we started contributed greatly to our progress with that quarry. The pain of the quarry abated. One of the amazing human qualities is the ability to adapt both passively as well as actively to adverse conditions and we certainly adapted. Adaptation was not easy or smooth and I still shudder whenever I think of what went on there in the Quarry. Then there were the bouts of depression, but this receded. It was largely during those hard years in that quarry that our brotherhood was consolidated and further contributed to our ultimate triumph. Today there is a warm bond between us irrespective of political organization. We are all proud of the achievements of Stephen Tshwete, Dikgang Moseneke, Stanley Mogoba, Jacob Zuma, Ibrahim Ibrahim (whom we knew as Chota) etc.

Much later (in 2003) when I learnt that our prison files were transferred to the National Archives in Pretoria I went to look up my files and I was not too amazed to learn that the Prison Department had some parody of a 'rehabilitation programme' for us with regular reports to a Prison Board. My report to the Prison Board stated that I was "lui, sorgloos en nalatig in sy werk" (lazy, negligent and careless in his work), "kan met niks vertrou word nie" (cannot be trusted with anything) and "sy gedrag is swak en vorme van disipline verset hy hom " (his behaviour is bad and he is resistant to all forms of discipline), moet geskors word (should be fired). With such a report I should have been evicted from the quarry but the part that recommended that I be expelled from the 'workshop' (read Quarry) was left blank. The careless and negligent part still intrigues me. How can one be negligent with stones.

Later during the reign of colonel Badenhorst I was promoted to a stone dresser in the quarry. I was paid the princely sum of fifty cents per month. I had great difficulty even with this work. I could just 'dress' a flat stone. A corner stone was a sheer impossibility. A flat stone was supposed to have one flat surface and a corner stone three smoothed surfaces at ninety degrees to each other. Delport was very watchful and came along and inspected each stone, made his mark on it and registered it in his book against the name of the prisoner who dressed it. He wanted to fire me. Anthony Suze, who was an expert, tried hard to teach me how to dress stones. He gave up and made extra stones for me to register. Klaas Mashishi who was another incompetent academic trying to dress stones made the same arrangement with Tony. James Marsh who became another stone dressing expert also provided extra stones to the incompetents. I was finally fired back to the wheelbarrows but later again brought back to the stone dresser span.

After about six years in the quarry the mean and brutish Delport was, starting to undergo a character change and we were increasingly engaging him in discussions sometimes ending in him swearing. He eventually decided to study and was looking for help with his studies. I think us getting on with our studies and his realization that he was at a dead-end in his rank must have contributed to his desire to study. He must have become aware of our successes in our studies. I was by that time a bit of an expert on the Bible, having read and re-read it during solitary confinement days and I was able to engage Delport in Biblical knowledge. I think Tony Suze and also Ernest Malgas contributed much to the change in Delport. Tony was already teaching him English and helping him with his other School Leaving Certificate subjects.

The quarry changed when Delport started to study. The atmosphere gradually became more relaxed. We now went out to the quarry to bask in the sun. In the mornings we collected tools not to work but to stand or sit around the whole day discussing Economics, Science, Politics and Philosophy. The quarry as our university became easier. Soccer tactics for the forthcoming matches were also planned there. The holiday type atmosphere spread to other Working Spans.

The change in Delport when it finally came was thus no less than a miracle.

I think this truly remarkable change in Delport started a few years earlier. I knew this because Delport refrained from reporting our clandestine activities in the quarry to the Prison Security. During that time Bra Jeff and I were experimenting with the screw jack to push the bars at the cell window apart and Bra Jeff was also busy designing a quick fit rafts, Delport must have recognized the raft. It consisted of a frame in which to slip two forty-four gallon drums which would give the necessary buoyancy Delport once casually remarked to Bra Jeff, completely out of the blue and with no preamble, that we must remember that the sea was sometimes very cold.

I think the more moderate policies of colonel Badenhorst who became the commanding officer later must also have had something to do with the change in prison conditions because a Head Warder Gloyne was put in charge of the yard and he took things easy as well. Lt Munro who became the Head of the Prison before Fourie also had a less physical and more psychological approach to retribution for opposing his government. Fourie himself was more liberal. The efforts of Mrs. Helen Suzman and the International Red Cross must also not be forgotten.

News of the new atmosphere must have reached the then Head of the Prison, however, who did not like this change and one day we found Delport transferred to a different section of the Island and replaced by a new head warder who tried his best to change the quarry back to a place of hard and useless labour. The story went around that the Head of the Prison on his rounds caught the Bamboo Span (the sea weed collecting span) sleeping at their place of work. The warder in charge of the span had parked his rifle against a tree and also stretched himself out to sleep. Both warder and prisoners were caught and charged and all work groups including the quarry were thereafter 'inspected' regularly. By that time I was working in the Prison Library and I missed the fun.

Getting work in the Prison Library was another miracle. I, with the help of the International Red Cross, got permission to re-organize the prison Library. This took me out of the quarry causing a pain with a number of Warders especially Head Warder Smith who was then in charge of the Yard. I was studying for a degree in Library and Information Science and this was an additional motivation to be allowed to re-organize the Prison Library.

I later learnt that Delport was finally promoted from Head Warder to Chief Warder. I saw him walking proudly displaying the Chief Warder insignia in the crook of his arm. Shortly after his promotion he left Robben Island Prison. I wonder what eventually happened to him.

Chapter 13

Release and Banned

The last six months in prison were very difficult. On the one hand there was the impending break of friendships developed over almost thirteen years and on the other hand relief from a very hostile environment and the excitement of entering a new. Furthe, our Community was split and in trouble. The Island was in turmoil. There was an influx of very naïve youngsters, some still boisterous and others very subdued, the latter claiming that they were just picked up by the police, not having been involved in anything. The agreement that was informally entered into between the factions in the prison, was not to recruit new comers to political organizations until they settled in, was broken. There was thus so much to do to repair the breakdown in the community. At the same time I had to start thinking about the outside world where the real issues pertaining to democratization of South Africa would face me and I had apprehensions about how I would adapt. Would I recognize my family and friends and would they still be friends now that I have acquired a stigma and what tasks would be required of me. At times during the last days on the Island the impending separation from comrades who had become much more than friends was more frightening than the uncertainties of what awaited me after release.

I was eventually released at the end of September 1977, but I was not going to be allowed even the semi freedom my fellow citizens who were not white were allowed to have in Apartheid South Africa. I was met at the Cape Town harbour by the Security Police who took me off to their Cape Town Headquarters in Caledon Square where it all started so many years ago. My family was not informed of my release. At the Police Headquarters I was handed a set of "banning orders" signed by the minister of justice, which amongst other things prohibited me from taking up any teaching post, entering any school or factory premises, 'absenting myself from the Magisterial Area of Cape Town', speaking to more than one person at a time, reporting to the Police every Wednesday, entering a residential area besides Bo-Kaap etc. The boundaries of the magisterial area of Cape Town were not specified and nobody seemed to know where this was. My lawyers had to get this from the State Library. This banning order lasted for another seven years. The appearance of the Security Police office did not seem to have changed since I was there last and I could not help apprehensively looking around for the chalk circle, the rubber batons, pliers and the electricity generator and the other tools of the trade of the Security Branch Police.

The physical feature of 'the outside world' that struck me most when I finally had a chance to look around my new environment was the appearance of size. Everything – the buildings, the doors, the cars, looked so peculiarly small – like toy houses and toy cars. Cars, radios, televisions, seemed excessively noisy and irritating. I had to relearn how to plot my way across streets and roads. Even one car in the road seemed dangerous and I remembered how amused a gang of idlers on the corner of Leeuwen and Bryant streets found me trying to cross the street.

Having lived in such close proximity with others for so long, life in 'normal' society with all its noise and activities was at first exceedingly lonely. I felt anxious and I half expected somebody to come, walk and peregrinate with me up and down the street gently inviting me to talk about my problems or just walk quietly with me (i.e. take me on the taxi) as we did with fellow prisoners during their periods of depression, which we all went through at one time or another during our stay on Robben Island (i.e. our 'cracking' periods o the "Period of Sounds as Des Brutus called it).

During those early days of my release my thoughts continually went back to my comrades on Robben Island and I could not help worrying about them. It took some time for me to realize that my Island Days had come to an end, that the years of prohibition and banning had started and that I must look forward to the future and what I could contribute to the task of achieving a democracy and freeing our people from the yoke of poverty.

I am often asked if I suffer any long term aftereffects of prison. Besides the physical, the most distressing after effect for me is my loss of geographic orientation. Before prison I was able to find my way to every nook and cranny in Cape Town. Today even though I have been back in Cape Town for more than thirty years, I might get lost even a few streets from my home and I have to ask for directions. I remember one day wandering alone in a mall in Johannesburg. I had lost my way back to the hotel and spent more than three hours trying to find the path back, despite getting directions from people I met in the mall. Fortunately there now exists the GPS and I have three of these devices). I also still get visual disturbances when parts of my visual field gets blocked out and replaced with jagged flashes of black and white, very reminiscent of the after effects of security police assisted sleep deprivation episodes. The vivid dreams of prison have fortunately diminished but it is still intrudes into my dreams.   Other effects of long term incarceration listed in textbooks such as chronophobia, listlessness, mental vacuity did not affect me (or so I think).

The first problem after my release was getting a job. My mother was staying with my brother who was not working and I was expected to join them and contribute the household expenses.

Teaching was out of the question since the banning order expressly prohibited me from "entering any place which constitutes the premises on which any public or private university, university college, college, school or other educational institution is situated or teaching anyone except my immediate children and it is not clear if this includes grandchildren.

I was also prohibited from entering the Supreme or Magistrate courts except as a defendant.

I wanted to continue with the M.Sc. degree I tried to start while in prison. The other option was to continue my study overseas.

Other study possibilities were Sweden, Germany or Britain. Arrangements for study were already made in Germany and in Sweden. The problem was the passport and consideration of where most anti apartheid struggle activity was centred, since I also wanted to join this abroad.

I applied for permission to attend the University of Cape Town.

On 7 November I received a letter from the Chief Magistrate of Cape Town in response to my application informing me that:

"with further reference to your letter of 5 October 1977 I have to inform you that the Honourable Minister of Justice has refused your application to attend the University of Cape Town during the academic year of 1978"

I nevertheless managed to register for an M.Sc degree by meeting lecturers off campus mostly in the Cape Town Botanical Gardens since I was not allowed to enter university premises but there were other problems. In fact the prohibition from the Apartheid Government now also expressly forbade me from registering at the University of Cape Town.   Since the banning order also expressly prohibited the "preparing, compiling, printing, publishing, disseminating or transmitting in any manner whatsoever any publication", doing a research degree was thus problematic.   Even attendance at an academic or scientific meeting or the writing up of a scientific paper or report needed permission from the minister.

Getting a job was thus immensely difficult in the face of the banning orders. Companies were nervous and easily intimidated by the Security Police. I nevertheless applied for teaching posts. The Catholic School in Athlone was prepared to offer me a teaching post but I could not get a variation in the banning order even to visit the school. The next job I tried was in Librarianship since I also had a degree in this field. The Cape Town City Council had no vacancies even though the leadership of the Municipal Workers Union indicated that this was not true. Posts at the university had two problems. The banning order did not allow me to enter any educational institution and the university was outside the magisterial area to which I was confined.

When a vacancy as a Statistician became available at the Medical Research Council, I applied. The Medical Research Council is outside the Cape Magisterial area and again I had to apply for permission to absent myself from the area to go for an interview and again my application was rejected.   In the meantime I was selling eggs for a living. The local newspaper published a picture showing me selling eggs in the streets with a caption as the best qualified egg seller in Cape Town.

I also did mathematics tutoring as a means of supplementing our meagre income but this was also prohibited under the banning orders. The students had to be careful not to be seen entering my house. One day the security police arrived just before my class assembled and Maraldea, who usually sat outside on the porch of Mrs Patience, our neighbour as guard, warned the students. The Police entered our house and when they   noticed Maraldea's absence they asked after her and I told them that she was next door watching television. They then offered to provide us with a television. I wonder what devices would have been fitted inside this television.

Maraldea, the nurse who started a correspondence with me whilst I was on the Island, had come back from Britain. Our correspondence started in 1966 after first Sonny Singh and then Aaron Gokwana went for medical treatment to Somerset Hospital. Sonny for the bash against the head he got in the Stone Quarry and Aaron to have his lung deflated as treatment for the TB he acquired in prison. Both of them met Maraldea at the Hospital and came to tell me about her when they returned to the Island. Sonny did not speak to her. She thought that the knock to the head might have disorientated him but when he came back he told me that he met her. Aaron on the other hand declared to her that I was his teacher and was prepared to smuggle a letter in to me from her, which she wisely declined.

After talking to them I ventured my next letter to her at Somerset Hospital not sure whether she would receive it. The letter was precious since we were allowed to write a letter once every six months and as an E-group prisoner I had no letter that previous year. The letter was sent and, I later learnt, caused quite a stir at the hospital because of the prison stamps all over the 'envelope'. She later told me that everybody at the hospital read it. It became a sort of public property. Her letter on the other hand was also read by everybody on my side despite the holes and blacked out lines by the censor office to stop me getting any 'unauthorized' news and information from the outside world.

Maraldea came back about a year before my release and we restarted our correspondence with her using an address of one of her white patients.

I met Maraldea in November of the year of my release and despite the banning order we started going out together. She taught me to drive a car again. The event that happened during our courtship that she remembers the best was when we went to see Edith Piaff at the Little Theatre and when, during the performance I whispered to her that I forgot to report to the Police that day as required by the banning order. She could not attend to the rest of the performance because of the mounting anxiety she experienced. She said that she began wondering what she would have to tell my mother if I was arrested for failing to report. I nevertheless went in to report at the police station. This failure to report on time was conveyed to the Security Police who immediately came to visit me the following day with dire threats. I was told that if I transgress again I will be arrested immediately.

Despite the banning order I sometimes joined Maraldea's family on picnics but had to hide on the floor of the car along the route but we never went further than Hout Bay.

We eventually got married in 1979. The marriage process was another issue. I had to get permission from the minister of justice to include Maraldea in the list of people that I was allowed to be associated with. Then there was the problem of the ceremony and the reception. The banning order prohibited me from "attending any social gathering, that is to say, any gathering at which the persons present also have social intercourse with one another" I was told that I would not be allowed to have a reception but my lawyer said that they could not stop my mother from having the reception at our house unless they ban her as well. The letter from the Magistrate finally allowing all this is given below

We found a house in Salt River for rent and I had to get a ministerial permit to change my address. Fortunately Salt River is still in the Cape Magisterial Area otherwise we would have had problems but I still required permission to relocate since the banning order prohibited me

§ 418

Telegramadres: "LANDDROS"
Telegraphic Address: "MAGISTRATE"

Telefoonnommer 41-1711
Telephone No.

Privaatsak 9017
Private Bag No.

Poskode 8000
Postal Code

DEPARTEMENT VAN JUSTISIE—DEPARTMENT OF JUSTICE
REPUBLIEK VAN SUID-AFRIKA—REPUBLIC OF SOUTH AFRICA

Verwysingsnommer
Reference No.

11/5/2 = 104

LANDDROSKANTOOR
MAGISTRATE'S OFFICE

CAPE TOWN

1978.12.19

Mr S Isaacs

51 Leeuwen Street

CAPE TOWN

8000

Sir

RELAXATION OF RESTRICTIONS

1. With further reference to my evenly numbered minute of the
    11th instant I have to inform you that permission is granted
    for you to attend the ceremony on the occasion of your
    marriage to Mareldia Davids at the Kensington Mosque at
    9th Street, Kensington, at about 14h00 on 1978.01.05 subject
    to the following conditions:

    (a) that you follow the shortest route from your residence
        to the Mosque and back

    (b) that you enter Kensington for the sole purpose of getting
        married

    (c) that you do not communicate with other listed communists
        or restricted persons

    (d) that you adhere to all other conditions of the restric-
        tion orders in force against you.

2. You are also allowed to receive and have guests at your
    house after the marriage until 21h00 on 1978.01.05 subject
    to the conditions in paragraph 1 (c) and (d) above.

3. It is accepted that after your marriage your wife will be a
    member of your household.

Yours faithfully

MAGISTRATE OF CAPE TOWN

Fig 9. Letter granting permission to have a wedding reception

from "entering any area set apart under any law for the occupation of Black,Coloured or Asiatic persons, except Schotshekloof" where my mother was staying. (The banning order strangely did not prohibit me from entering an area 'set aside for Whites').

One of the wedding presents we received was a weekend in Pniel, which happened to be more than thirty kilometers outside the magisterial area to which I was confined, but we decided to risk it. We just had to be careful and be back before the following Wednesday. On the second day of our stay the area was suddenly swarming with police and I had the vision of going back to prison. I went to hide and Maraldea went to find out details and learnt that some prisoners had escaped from the nearby prison and the police and warders were hunting them.

The first person to come and visit us there in Burns Road Salt River was Meldin Pistoli who had been released from Robben Island just after me. He was not banned but was banished to some obscure area in Transkei. The two of us speaking to one another was a criminal offence in terms of the Apartheid Government law for both of us but this was not easy to prove unless we were arrested in the act or 'red handed' but absenting

himself from his place of banishment was easy to prove. He was consequently arrested on his return to Transkei, charged for absenting himself from the area in Transkei and sentenced to three months in prison.

Subsequent visits from ex-prisoners to me were much more discrete and carefully managed by Maraldea. The Security Police also visited us regularly and one day Maraldea noticed that after visiting us they called in at the house directly opposite us, the house of an ex-railway pensioner. Perhaps the pensioner was recruited to watch us or perhaps it was just an attempt at intimidation. It never really bothered us.

Fig 10 Tony Suze after his release

We were both beyond the age of thirty and planned to have our children as soon as possible. Maraldea was then working for both of us but when she became pregnant she threatened to abort our child right from the third month and had to give up working. I started selling eggs again and tried working as a handyman in the area to eke out a meagre existence there in Salt River. Later our income was supplemented from a donation from the Anglican Church in Britain and the International Red Cross and an additional food parcel during Islamic festive days. In July 1979 our first child, a daughter was born. Our second child was born in 1981.

My need to spend time in a well equip academic library made me sneak out of the magisterial district to go to the University of Cape Town library. One day as I crossed the M5 (Settler's Way) which was the boundary of the Magisterial Area of Cape Town, a member of the Security Police drove past and saw me but I did not see him. He made a u-turn to arrest me but I, having noticed a low fuel level, drove down a side street to look for a petrol station. After buying a supply of petrol I drove further out of the magisterial district to the university library. He must have thought I was trying to dodge him and he immediately drove to my place of residence in Burns Road to wait for me and to ask my wife where I was. She told the Security Police that I had gone to visit my mother in Bo-Kaap.

When I arrived back home Maraldea told me about the visit from the Police. The Police told Maraldea to tell me to report to the Police Head quarters at Caledon Square. I was not aware that they saw me outside the magisterial area and I thought that their visit had to do with my application to take up a scholarship in Germany. It was thus with great anticipation that I went to Caledon Square and the disappointment was thus not unexpected when told that I was being arrested for absenting myself from the Magisterial Area of Cape Town. I received a formal charge sheet that gave the date of my appearance in court. I was told that the Police generously would not oppose bail. I took the charge sheet to our lawyer Mr. Dallah Omar who appointed Advocate De La Hunt to defend me and supported by the organisation known as the Defence and Aid from Britain.

The case was postponed about three times and when a final date was set my good friend Jamaal Hamdulay from SASA (South African Students Association) offered to be my star witness. He said that he would testify that he used our car the morning the police saw it crossing the Cape Magisterial boundary. He d no respect for the Apartheid government and their courts.

The Security Police must have seen Jamaal sitting outside the court waiting to be called in because they hastily went to arrest Jamaal's foreman from work to testify that the person sitting outside the court by the name of Jamaal Hamdulay never left his place of work and therefore could not have been the person driving my car on the day it was observed. Maraldea quietly left the courtroom to go and warn Jamaal. Jamaal brushed this warning off saying he would deal with that situation. In court when he was challenged by the foremen's testimony Jamaal said that that foreman did not know any thing and that it was very easy to dodge out of the workplace and that he has witnesses to testify to this. He also testified that he had borrowed my car to take his wife to the St Monica's maternity home on Signal hill and left her there and then went right across the city to Mowbray to buy a newspaper. I thought that this was indeed a very unlikely story but it was not questioned in court. The case against me was then dismissed, not because I was not guilty but because of insufficient evidence.

Jamaal was subsequently arrested and thrown in a police cell. In the cell Jamaal got up and sat down to pray. When the police observed this through the Judas Hole in the cell door, they burst in and accused Jamaal of hypocrisy trying to pray and the other day blatantly lying in court.

Despite the banning orders a steady stream of ex-prisoners and other activist visited me always with Maraldea maintaining security.

In 1981 I finally got a job that fitted some of my academic qualifications. There was a vacancy in the Porphyria research laboratory and I was a likely candidate. The police arrived at the laboratory and must have convinced the head that I was not a suitable person to be employed there. Fortunately a vacancy as a Statistician was available in the Computer Services Department at Groote Schuur Hospital and the Head of the Hospital Dr H R Sanders was able to resist the police threats and warnings. The Police were given the impression that the job would not involve any contact with other employees, patients or the public. I would only be counting patients and writing computer programmes. The job was actually a joint post with the University of Cape Town and involved an extensive consulting service with postgraduate students and the staff involved in research. I consulted our advocate for an opinion as to whether I was breaking the banning orders by working for the Hospital and the University. This consultation was deemed necessary should I be arrested and charged for contravening the banning orders. His opinion was that the hospital could not be regarded as university property. It was left at that but later I discovered, in some obscure archives, that the grounds on which the hospital was built was in fact also university property and that the hospital was supposed to pay a rental of R2.00 per annum. This would have given me serious problems if the police came across this. The issue of working meetings was again brought up. If more than one person entered the office where I was working then I could only speak to one at a time. If there was a common purpose or concerted action then the presence of the third person became illegal and I could be charged with contravening the banning order. I nevertheless started work and started seeing students.

I never told anybody from the hospital or the university that I was banned and only senior management knew my history. I was later promoted to the post of Specialist Scientist. Ex prisoners came to visit me regularly in secret at my office in the hospital.

I eventually became the Head of the Department, after it changed its name to Medical Informatics. After the banning order expired I was elected president of the South African Health Informatics Association and helped build the African Region of the International Medical Informatics Association (IMIA). I was subsequently elected Honorary Fellow of the International Medical Informatics Association for outstanding contribution to Medical and Health Informatics.

My banning order finally expired in 1986 and in 1990 I obtained a visa to undertake a sabbatical in Germany. After more than twenty years I finally became as 'free' as my fellow disenfranchised people of South Africa. It was then finally possible to complete a PhD with the help of DAAD (the German Academic exchange programme). I spent three months at Philips University in Marburg Germany. I was then elected fellow of the Royal Statistical Society and a chartered member of the British Computer Society. In 2010 I was elected as honorary fellow of the International Medical Informatics Association in recognition for contributions to Medical Informatics. In 2011 I was nominated as 'Companion of Demontford University in the UK.

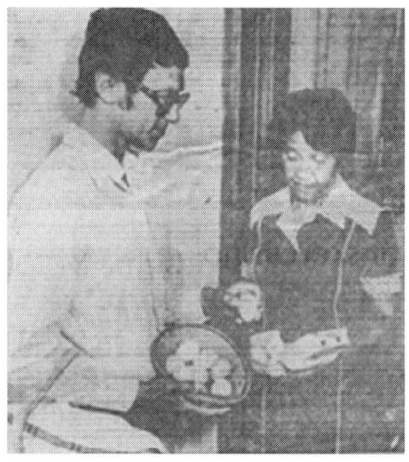

Fig 11 Selling eggs for a living (Cape Argus)

In 2010 I was nominated "Sports Icon" by the Department of Arts, Culture and Sport for my contributions to Sport on Robben Island

My own children discovered my history only when they saw an exhibition of ex-Robben Island prisoners at the National Museum and was amazed to see my handwriting there.

I retired in 2005 and continued with some consulting in Statistics and some tutoring in Mathematics at various school levels in Cape Town and more recently in Khayelitsha. In 2009 I worked for the police setting up an information system and experienced the irony of working for an organization that so abused me in the past. Of course the police are now regarded as our own and not as the apartheid police of the past.

I think I have since overcome the main after-effects of the discomforts I experienced at the hands of the police and in prison but my wife thinks I should still go and see a psychologist.

What pains me the most today is that the hard nosed comrades I lived with and who were so concerned with the welfare of the oppressed and who subsequently found their way into government, have allowed South Africa to become the most economically disparate society (in terms of Geni Index) in the world. I also cannot understand how these hard-nosed, streetwise politicians were conned into buying such extremely expensive white elephants, in the form of warships and warplanes, in the face of so much poverty and the rising infant mortality in our country reaching a level even worse than Afghanistan.